Dawning of Clear Light

Other books by Martin Lowenthal

Embrace Yes: The Power of Spiritual Affirmation

Opening the Heart of Compassion: Transform Suffering Through Buddhist Psychology and Practice
(with Lar Short)

Dawning of Clear Light

A Western Approach
to
Tibetan Dark Retreat Meditation

Martin Lowenthal

HAMPTON ROADS
PUBLISHING COMPANY, INC.

Cover design by Grace Pedalino
Cover photography by Photodisc © 2003
Interior illustrations by Anne L. Louque

Hampton Roads Publishing Company, Inc.
1125 Stoney Ridge Road
Charlottesville, VA 22902

434-296-2772
fax: 434-296-5096
e-mail: hrpc@hrpub.com
www.hrpub.com

If you are unable to order this book from your local
bookseller, you may order directly from the publisher.
Call 1-800-766-8009, toll-free.

Library of Congress Cataloging-in-Publication Data

Lowenthal, Martin.
  Dawning of clear light : a western approach to Tibetan dark retreat
meditation / Martin Lowenthal.
      p. cm.
Includes bibliographical references and index.
  ISBN 1-57174-375-8 (alk. paper)
  1. Meditation--Bonpo (Sect) 2. Rdzogs-chen (Bonpo) 3. Bonpo
(Sect)--Doctrines. I. Title.
  BQ7982.2.L68 2003
  299'.54--dc21
                                                    2003010770

                    ISBN 1-57174-375-8

                  10 9 8 7 6 5 4 3 2 1

        Printed on acid-free paper in the United States

Dedication

With gratitude to Tenzin Wangyal Rinpoche, who introduced me to dark retreats and who has supported my non-traditional work with them, and to Lopon Tenzin Namdak, whose presence and teachings continue to be a profound transmission and inspiration.

In memory of my mother, Juliet.

May this humble effort be of benefit to all and support the growth, happiness, and freedom of all living beings.

Table of Contents

Foreword
by Tenzin Wangyal Rinpoche

It is wonderful that Martin, a long-time, dedicated practitioner who is exploring his own way in the spiritual path, is offering this unique guide to the dark retreat. His wealth of personal experience and insight lends a great deal of guidance and support to other individuals who are in a journey to discovering and abiding in the light that can be found within the darkness.

The dark retreat has been a very important, secret practice in the traditional Dzogchen teachings for thousands of years, both within the Nyingma school of Tibetan Buddhism and the Bön tradition of Tibet. It is important for practitioners of Dzogchen to prepare themselves by receiving and following complete instructions according to the teachings. These teachings require the student to complete a variety of practices, including ngondro, powa, introduction to the nature of mind, and various stability practices, before formally engaging in the dark retreat.

It is very hard for individuals in our Western culture to do everything as it has traditionally been done. Therefore, Martin's book opens a door to having some exposure to experiences of one's self in the absence of all the visual and sensory stimulation of day-to-day life. A retreat in complete darkness effectively takes the remote control out of one's hands, leaving one witness to the blank screen of one's own mind. This book offers welcome access to the experience of one's self in a variety of ways during dark retreat.

—Tenzin Wangyal Rinpoche

Acknowledgments

A book, like a dark retreat, is a community effort. I am profoundly grateful to all my teachers and all their teachers who have passed down the great teachings and practices for thousands of years. Thanks also to all the students associated with the Dedicated Life Institute who have supported my retreats, done retreats of their own, and who make it possible to carry these traditions forward for future generations.

I want to thank Jerome Petiprin for his commentary and feedback on the early version of the manuscript. I am also deeply grateful to my wife, Karen Edwards, for her support during retreats and her help in editing the first draft of this book. I owe thanks to Annemie Curlin for her assistance in my translation of Rainer Maria Rilke. And great gratitude to Grace Pedalino at Hampton Roads Publishing for her willingness to champion this book, her editing, and her support throughout the entire process of bringing this work to the public.

My most profound gratitude goes to the Sacred, which gives and serves all life and is such an intimate presence in the dark.

Introduction

Even the darkness is not too dark for Thee,
But the night shineth as the day;
The darkness is even as the light.

—Psalms, 139:12

Retreats in darkness have been used by all the great spiritual traditions for thousands of years as a method for tapping deep clarity, accessing sacred wisdom, connecting with the Divine, and training to transform the mind/body system into a manifestation of wisdom. In Tibetan Buddhism and Bön, the teachings and practices of dark retreat have been passed down through the ages and are taught and practiced today.

Darkness As a Setting

Dark retreats are both a setting for doing meditation practice and a specific practice environment for Dzogchen teachings in the Bön and Nyingma lineages of Tibet. In the dark, the seamless unity of space provides an environment for realizing the seamless unity of experience. The thoughts that arise are clearly the product of the differentiating conceptual mind and their transient, insubstantial nature is more apparent. The dark provides a profound opportunity to recognize our true nature and realize that our experiences are simply reflections of that nature. The resulting clarity can lead to the realization of profound wisdom, unshakable presence, spontaneous freedom from our mental/emotional habits, transformation of the ordinary into wisdom, and abiding in a state of Clear Light.

The dark is a kind of womb in which to grow into a new way of being. The particular advantages of the dark are many. The rest for our eyes, weary from overstimulation in our visually oriented world, promotes an overall relaxation of body and mind. Living in the dark changes the body chemistry, particularly the pineal, pituitary, thalamus, and hypothalamus glands. The less frequently used senses of hearing and touch expand in importance as we mindfully operate in ways adapted to functioning without the use of sight. The life is simple, allowing for more time and effort to be concentrated on practice. Without the stimulation of external light, the conditions are improved for seeing the inner lights, and it is easier to observe the thought patterns that arise out of the internal dynamics of our own minds. The visions and thoughts in the dark tell us what life is like in the unnoticed regions of our being. And the darkness is both intimate and boundless simultaneously.

Tibetan Bön Dzogchen and Dark Retreat

In the Bön tradition of Tibet, dark retreat is considered one of the most powerful and suitable environments for working with the teachings of Dzogchen, the practice of the nature of mind. Dzogchen works with the essence of all being and that which is beyond everything. It is often referred to as the direct path of liberation in which we are able to recognize the open nature of experience. We see each experience exactly as it is, without treating it as having power of its own or requiring any response.

Dzogchen is a view of reality that is based on a profound understanding of the nature of all being, awareness, and experience. This nature of all being, awareness, and experience is called the nature of mind, and the pure awareness of this nature is called "Clear Light." The mind of Clear Light is totally open, boundlessly and unwaveringly radiant, and unreservedly inclusive.

In the teachings, a distinction is made between clarity and Clear Light. Often the open presence of the sense of witness or hosting everything that arises is referred to as clarity. The sense of presence is open, inclusive, and beyond the personal.

Clear Light refers to abiding in an open, nondual awareness beyond any distinction between self and object. In Clear Light all there is, is is. It is beyond experience and experiencer, beyond thinking and not thinking, beyond subject and object.

I was introduced to dark retreats as a practice by Tenzin Wangyal Rinpoche as part of his teachings of the Experiential Transmission of the *Zhang Zhung Nyan Gyud*. I hosted his trips to Boston each year for these teachings beginning in 1993. Even though the prescribed forty-nine-day dark retreat comes at the end of the cycle of eight teachings, he introduced short dark retreats early in the series as a way to support the practice and to familiarize students with the conditions of doing a retreat in darkness. Years previous to this, I had learned of short dark retreats from Namkhai Norbu Rinpoche in his teachings on Dzogchen.

The first year of the Experiential Transmission teachings involved a Ngondro[1] (preparation practices which include guru yoga,[2] dedication, impermanence practices, offering of body and mind, mandala, and other practices that are considered foundational or preliminary to Dzogchen). The second year we were introduced to dark retreat and sky-gazing practices.

In dark retreat, the practitioner lives in complete darkness—eating, sleeping, meditating, and simply existing in a world without external light. The journey of the dark retreat is made through silence, in silence, and into the profound silence from which all sound arises.

The purposes of the dark retreat according to this tradition are to relax, cut through mental/emotional habits, harmonize the elements in the body, work with visions, and simply rest in the "Natural State."

My experience in my first three-day dark retreat was so profound that I have continued to do them at least once a year since then, usually for a number of weeks. In this process, the practices and purposes of the retreats have evolved based on deeper understandings of the teachings and out of my own experience as a Western practitioner and teacher.

Dark Retreat As Context for Practicing Mindfulness and Tantra

Many of the teachings related to dark retreat address the need for calming the mind, dealing with disturbances and obstacles, and balancing the elements. Various forms of mindfulness practice are part of addressing this need. These can include simple zhiné (shamatha)[3] practice to concentrate and stabilize our attention in calm abiding, as well as more open forms of Vipashyana[4] that involve the clear intuitive recognition of impermanence and the insight into the open nature of being and awareness.

In a sense, mindfulness is the simultaneous practice of concentration, the ability to stabilize the mind in a state without distraction, and decentration, the ability to open attention to whatever is arising.

Dark retreat is also a conducive and powerful setting for practicing tantra. In Austria in 1991, Lopon Tenzin Namdak gave teachings on dark retreat in the tradition that comes from the *Dzogchen yangtse klongchen*. In these practices, visions are purified by way of the five Buddha fields and the five Dhyani Buddhas. In the darkness we discover the radiance of wisdom of each of these Buddhas. He noted that the methods of these practices are close to the methods of tantra.

With my background in both Buddhist tantra and Taoist inner alchemy, I have found the dark particularly useful in these practices. Tantra is a path of inner alchemy and transformation. It uses the body, the emotions, sound, movement, and the imagination to transform the ordinary into something of value—wisdom, love, compassion, and beauty. It involves retraining the body's habitual reactions through the cultivation of our wisdom nature.

Tantra uses imagination, senses, and creativity to transform experience into food for the spirit. This is a kind of alchemy. Every act of creating value from the material of life—thoughts, sensations, emotions, energies—is a kind of tantra. The tantras of Tibet are a developed form of alchemy that use attention, light, color, sound, sensation, and imagination to create the conditions for the alchemical process to occur. When that happens, the sense of presence is intensified, perceptions change, and our relationship to the world shifts.

The principles of tantric transformation are implicit in true spiritual dedication, whether one follows a set of "tantric" practices or not. Dedicating each moment, action, and one's life to a sacred purpose, spiritual growth, and/or embodying a sacred wisdom quality is a form of tantra. The acts of writing poetry, creating visual beauty, and making music are all transformative processes. When done as part of self and collective cultivation, they are tantric.

For example, in dark retreat I have not only benefited from formal tantric practices, but also have found that writing—poetry, stories, dreams, teachings—has been a powerful part of the work of opening my heart. My writing is a spiritual practice, an engagement with creative and wisdom energies that open me to the unknown and shape me as I work.

Dark Retreat in the Overall Picture of Meditation and Spiritual Work

All of the practices being discussed can be thought of as part of a path of meditation (in the broadest sense of this word). Essentially, the aim of meditation is to awaken our aliveness with clarity and authenticity, to use it for the direct and intuitive experience of reality, moment to moment, and to manifest this in the world as a beneficial presence in our relationships, our work, and in our community. Meditation is a path which acquaints the mind with our wisdom nature and cultivates the wisdom qualities of that essential nature as an authentic expression of our aliveness.

When we ask ourselves the question, "What is aliveness?" we intuitively know that the answer is not in chemical and physical definitions of the attributes of life. We sense that it has something to do with experience and the way we relate to experience.

Aliveness involves manifesting the energy of life as a way of being and as a presence in the world that others can experience. Aliveness is on the edge. Presence is the connectedness of that edge. Being is the ground that includes the edge and all that is not edge. Posture of the heart is the way we relate to ourselves and to the world.

Presence is made real and effective in our experience by remaining conscious in everything we do. We train ourselves to both radiate presence and behold and embrace the presence in everything around us, in trees, flowers, people, oceans, and in experience itself. And we abide in the splendor of that presence.

By committing to our growth and freedom beyond our hopes, fears, and identities and by transcending habitual ways of relating to ourselves, others, and life itself, we can live fully, contribute wisely, realize our dedication to being a beneficial presence, and create a sacred legacy. We can live each moment as a manifestation of our wisdom nature, as an expression of its creative flow, and as a celebration of life.

A main theme of this book is that we can develop greater clarity and awareness, moment to moment, in every context of life. We can become free of reactive habits of thought, feeling, and action, as our sense of presence, aliveness, and clarity manifests in whatever situations we encounter and whatever challenges we face.

The practices of the dark retreat also improve the quality of everyday life. While the greater goal is the realization and embodiment of wisdom, free from reactive habits and karmic traces, improving the conditions of daily living provides a more encouraging environment for continued practice.

A Western Practitioner's Experience
with Tibetan Teachings on Dark Retreat

This book presents teachings related to Dzogchen, Tantra, and dark retreat as well as selections from my journal of a month-long dark retreat in 1998, with added commentaries and lessons from my years of experience as a practitioner and teacher of meditation. I have also included a few selections from some of the ten other dark retreats I have done (the journals are indented and in a different typeface). The purpose is to share insights, to inspire, to give teachings, and to honor the divine energies that were my companions in solitude.

The teachings are meant as an introduction to the subject of spiritual work in dark retreat. I am not a scholar or an expert on traditional Tibetan teachings on dark retreat, although I have received many teachings from a number of accomplished, wondrous, and generous masters. I hope that the wonderful texts in the Tibetan traditions on this subject will someday be available in translation with commentaries by Tibetan masters. I can only authentically share based on my experience.

The journal selections are not intended to reveal the story of my life, even though I share my personal experiences of dark retreats. I have always hesitated to talk and write about myself, because as a teacher I believe the teachings and the larger contexts of our lives are where the true lessons reside. My story, however dramatic or heroic or mundane, must not distract from the real source of wisdom, nor diminish the beauty and radiance of true spiritual realization.

It is not as if I have not experienced drama or been the hero of my own personal history. At times in my life, I have struggled with awkwardness, acute asthma, addiction to medication, insecurity, depression, divorce, death of loved ones, no money, chronic physical health conditions, dangerous natural and political situations, unrequited love, and attempts to be a good husband, parent, teacher, writer, friend, and human being. I failed at many endeavors and succeeded in others. I have performed many things well, others poorly, some about average, and a few exceptionally. My life story is both significant to me and irrelevant in the larger scheme of things in which I am fundamentally a small part.

Some readers might find it strange that my teachings and writings blend traditional Tibetan teachings with my experience and perspectives as a modern Western practitioner. My work, encouraged by teachers such as Dilgo Khyentse Rinpoche and Tenzin Wangyal Rinpoche, has always been dedicated to practicing what works spiritually for me as a Westerner, distilling out the principles of the teachings and the experience of practice, and making these accessible to people living in the conditions of the modern world with its diversity of religions and cultures, its secular society, and its emphasis on laity.

This book is intended to present the teachings in an accessible way. Sharing my experiences, reflections, and writings puts flesh on the conceptual skeletal structure of the teachings. My experience has grown out of extensive practice in the eleven dark retreats that I have done over the last nine years, as part of my thirty-plus years of work with meditation and various spiritual teachers, primarily based in the Tibetan traditions. I have also guided eighteen students in dark retreats over these years.

My retreats differed in many ways from the traditional Tibetan Buddhist and Bön use of such retreats. While inspired by those teachings and often under the supervision of Tenzin Wangyal Rinpoche, the format, conditions, and practices were often adapted to fit my particular spiritual work at the time and the requirements and opportunities of my life.

In Tibet, dark retreats were done primarily by monks as part of their training and with the support of the monastery. I, on the other hand, am not a monk but a "householder," someone who works for a living, has a wife and children, and lives in the larger community. I, like many Western students, have a busy schedule and personal, family, and community responsibilities.

I was also introduced to meditation and spiritual work as an adult rather than as part of the process of growing up. I came to the endeavor of meditation many years ago as a product of the secular society without the benefit of a religious upbringing and the sense of sacred ritual. I have had to work hard to develop some level of sensitivity, sensibility, and skill in the importance and performance of sacred rituals. By the time I began spending days and weeks meditating in darkness, I was not new to retreats, having done solo retreats of varying lengths over the course of more than twenty years.

My teachings are not a translation or an American version of Tibetan practices, though I have incorporated many practices directly from the Tibetan tradition. In my writings and teachings, I examine what is needed, find what works, discover how it works, and make it accessible to others. I often incorporate many methods that I have learned or developed based in Western psychology, particularly developmental frameworks, and from therapeutic techniques which are effective in retraining habits of mind. I have not worried about whether there are equivalent approaches in any particular tradition.

In addition I have sought to use a vocabulary that more accurately reflects experience and the use of English as my native language. This is particularly true in part 3, where I lay out a framework for understanding the teachings.

This approach is also reflected by my attempt to use the word "mind" sparingly. It is a word that is overused in translations of Buddhist literature and it does not convey either the meaning of the principles, the useful distinctions that need to be comprehended, or the experience of practice. In English the word is too readily associated with mental process, thinking, and the brain, which are not usually the subject of the teachings. I will try to use words that convey finer distinctions in English such as attention, awareness, consciousness, being, existence, self-sense, and wisdom. In some instances the way "mind" is used in the literature refers to an ultimate nature, which in Western mystical traditions would be called the Divine, God, Ein Sof, Essence, or Spirit, and in Taoism the Tao.

Some would argue with the particulars of these terms, but sectarian debates about the meanings have never interested me. The main criteria must be the extent to which the word points in some useful way to the phenomenon being referred to. The key question is, "Does it support a view that leads to understanding and eventual realization in the experience of the practitioner?"

Over the years, I have received encouragement in my efforts, teachings, and writings from all my teachers, particularly my Tibetan mentors. I try to be true in my respect, gratitude, and connection to the teachers who have opened my heart and given me so many gifts.

In this book, I am attempting to hold the dual aspects of my personal experience on the one hand and the larger universal teachings about life and spiritual work on the other, always inviting you, the reader, to examine your own life. Hopefully, you will be challenged to engage in a process that will promote not only your own growth, but the celebration of life, the blessings of the world, and the larger stories that we are all a part of.

This book is a celebration, not a melodrama. It is an invitation to find the treasures that are hidden within your own world and the world around you. I wrote my first spiritual book on the Buddhist psychology of suffering and the meditative path through the worlds of pain to freedom. Since that time in the early 1990s, I have returned to themes of a previous decade and integrated joy with pain as a gateway into the spiritual. While I once referred to the type of meditation that I taught as "celebrational meditation," it is not always cheery. I have spent hours upon hours sitting in pain with a sense of hopelessness and with tears running down my checks and onto my legs, soaking the entire area in front of me. I have sat with frustration and grief as I cried, my nose ran, and my mouth drooled—what some call the "three waters." The physical pains in the knees, back, and neck, the emotions that erupt when given the time and openness, and the thought patterns which seem endless and obsessive are some of the energies of aliveness.

It is our heart posture, our basic attitude about life, self, others, and the world, that shapes how we relate to, use, and grow from what arises in life and spiritual work. Meditation is not about solving the problems of life. It is about being present with whatever arises from a dimension of being that includes problems and is not problematic, that includes pain and is not painful, that includes our thoughts and is not our thoughts, that includes our feelings and is not our feelings, that includes our personalities and identities and is neither, that includes us and is not only ours, that is both personal and totally beyond the personal.

I invite you to join me in a song of praise. I know there are violence, poverty, death, despair, cruelty, hatred, intolerance, hostility, dishonesty, greed, and indifference in the world. I also believe that injustice and poverty and disease must be confronted, and that spiritual work should not be an escape from this world. We want to be a beneficial presence and to make a supportive contribution. To make a supportive contribution, we must access our own profound wisdom nature and see it in the world around us. To access this wisdom nature, we must transcend personal agendas and train ourselves for service in the larger contexts of life. It is through praise, grief, gratitude, love, and wholehearted engagement that we remake ourselves into a wisdom bodymind.

Imagine what it would be like to gather all your likes and dislikes and to make something of beauty as an offering of celebration of the sacred. Imagine placing all your emotions—joy, anger, sadness, depression, frustration, love, passion, desire, fear, and longing—in the service of wisdom, not only to live life, but to experience being lived by life, to let your being, your soul, care for you. Do not solve the problems of life or resolve all the seemingly paradoxical and conflicting realities and competing feelings. Hold them all. Have their energies feed your sense of presence. Be present with it all, opening more and more, and even more, beyond what you thought was possible. The key is in presencing— not in whatever ideas you have, pills you want, actions you take or work you do to accomplish something.

During the retreat and in this writing, a great number of teachers, philosophers, and poets have informed and supported me through my experiences of them, their examples, and their own writings and teachings. In a sense, I enjoyed the company of many people such as Tenzin Wangyal, Tenzin Namdak, Dilgo Khyentse, Lar Short, Martín Prechtel, David Whyte, John O'Donohue, and many others. I have included some of their words and ideas in this book along with my own experiences and teachings as an invitation to you to include them in your own circle of spiritual friends.

Part I
Radiant Heart of Darkness

In this dark space
thoughts, feelings, and plans
have boundless room
and no place.

So I gaze into blank blackness
praising memories of light and sky
and settle into
this unknown darkness.

With gratitude for the pulsing in palms
and cool breeze of inhaling breath,
I sit poised on the edge of tears, bliss
and I know not what.

Looking into endless, embracing dark,
in this still moment

are these bright lights and inaudible sounds
plays of fancy
or the true nature
of a freshly opened heart?

—Martin Lowenthal

1 What Is a Dark Retreat?

A dark retreat is a solitary journey done in total darkness. The dark retreat facility usually consists of a room for meditation and sleeping and an adjacent or nearby bathroom. The duration of the retreat will often vary from a few days to forty-nine days, and even to years in the case of some yogis in the caves of Tibet.

The purpose of such retreats is to relax into the nature of our own being, allowing the mind to discover its natural awareness. In this relaxation we discover the essential qualities of authentic presence, inner lights and visions, the energies of aliveness, silence, and listening, and sacred wisdom. In time we adopt an open heart posture of praise, gratitude, love, compassion, and peace. To find that relaxation and experience that wisdom means confronting and transcending our core fears, unspoken longings, and patterns of denial and addiction.

In a dark retreat, the play of the bodymind is exposed more clearly, without the presence of the usual multitude of external stimuli. External darkness becomes a screen for the performance of the internal theater of images, stories, and reactions.

As we relax and practice free of distractions, the energy of aliveness in all its embodiments is revealed and amplified. All of our physical, mental, and emotional patterns can be seen clearly. We also can more readily sense the flows of energy in the body, the energy field of presence, and the qualities we share with all existence. The wisdom qualities of "being" become more evident. These qualities are uncovered, recognized, and then cultivated, not because of a sense of incompleteness but because of the natural impulse to share and manifest as a beneficial presence in the connections that we feel and that we come to know exist with all others.

In the dark retreat, all experiences arise within a basic sense of hosting awareness and dissolve back into the space of hosting without the hosting's being affected. Just as the dark is open and inclusive, so our own being can include everything in its open nature, in the space of its awareness. Everything that arises comes from that space, exists within its nature, and dissolves into the space.

A way to think about this might be to imagine an empty room. A bed and desk are placed in the room. The space in the room is not diminished by the furniture. The space is the same before the furniture is moved in, while the bed and desk are in the room, and after they are removed.

The key aspect of this realization is that our basic nature is not affected, diminished, or enhanced by what we think, do, or say and that all thoughts, deeds, and expressions are natural reminders of our fundamental nature. What gets in our way are our habits of mind and reaction which hijack our attention away from our own natural way of being.

In these retreats, visions naturally arise and we learn to distinguish between those which are reactive projections of our body of habits, and those which are manifestations of our wisdom nature. We realize how all visions are a product of our minds.

The dark retreat is a safe space to practice and accelerate our relaxation into the sense of ease with the nature of being (nature of mind). For many, doing even a short dark retreat can bring about a significant shift in their lives, revealing another way of being, of relating to life, and of being present with oneself and one's own mind. We gradually enter into ourselves more completely, and at the same time, into all being.

2 Attitudes Toward Dark and Light

Darkness in a Bad Light

Orientation toward light in opposition to dark has characterized many periods of world history, many religions, and much of Western culture since the time of Plato more than 2,500 years ago. We seek physical light and light in our spiritual quests. Light is truly wondrous and transformative. The problem is the trivialization and often demonization of the dark. The dark represents the unknown, what we cannot understand, what we fear, what we repress and do not want to look at, what is uncomfortable, what is mysterious, and most prominently, death. It is often seen as the home of evil and sin, the source of violence, destruction, depression, and madness, and the destination of all who would remain ignorant.

Our desire to eliminate darkness takes both material and spiritual forms. The harnessing of electricity and the invention of the light bulb have not only extended our days and transformed our rhythms of work, they have deepened our preoccupation with external images, especially with the coming of television and computers. Many religions and cults seek to root out or suppress any and all hints of non-virtuous behavior and character in the quest for salvation through and into the light. Even many of our therapeutic psychologies see the dark or shadow as the abode or dimension of our personality that is the unacknowledged source of irrationality, suffering, and abusive behavior.

We pay for this exclusive orientation toward light with fear of the dark, a flight from mortality, and superficial lives relegated to experiencing only the surface of reality. This denial and fear of darkness lead to addictions that keep us from experiencing the discomfort and pain of depth. We numb ourselves with food, alcohol, and drugs, or we seek distraction through constant stimulation and entertainment. These habits also fuel the inevitable explosions of violence, depression, and madness that result from repression and indulgence, and the societal attempts to control such outbursts.

Our light-oriented rationality began at the time of Plato and, propelled by the European "Enlightenment," has tried to explain and conquer all mystery, and the sacred itself, in much the same way the West has subjugated lands and peoples. As Matthew Fox says, "we were robbed of savoring mystery and its darkness. We need to retrieve our rights to mystery and to the darkness in which it is so often immersed and enmeshed."[5]

Darkness in a Good Light
A Clear Midnight

This is thy hour O soul,
Thy free flight into the wordless,
Away from books, away from art,
The day erased, the lesson done,
Thee fully forth emerging, silent, gazing,
Pondering the themes thou lovest best:
Night, sleep, death and the stars.[6]

—Walt Whitman

7

We all began in the darkness of the womb. Our lives are sustained by organs that function in darkness. We probably conceived or will conceive our children in the intimacy of night, and our bodies will finish their cycles in the darkness of earth. The vegetation that nourishes us is germinated in the darkness of the ground. Nearly all space is dark, and it is theorized that our universe was birthed from darkness.

Running counter to the culture of darkness-denying light, many mystics and poets have extolled the virtue of darkness and its connection to the divine. From the Hebrew prophets and kabbalists, to ancient Greeks such as Parmenides and Pythagoras, to Meister Eckhart, to Rainer Maria Rilke, to many modern poets and writers, there runs a river of consciousness that perpetuates the path of descent into darkness and the fruit of wisdom that is given through that connection to God.

A common thread for these writers and teachers is the necessity of descending into the darkness to receive the gifts of wisdom and the blessings of the struggle with death and grief. This journey reveals our authentic relationship to the divine.

In speaking about darkness, Meister Eckhart said: "What is this darkness? What is its name? Call it: an aptitude for sensitivity. Call it: a rich sensitivity which will make you whole. Call it: your potential for vulnerability."[7] T. S. Eliot wrote: "I said to my soul, be still/ and let the dark come upon you/ which shall be the darkness of God."[8] David Whyte's poem *Sweet Darkness* points out:

Sometimes it takes darkness and the sweet
confinement of your aloneness

to learn anything or anyone
that does not bring you alive

is too small for you.[9]

3 The Goddess of the Dark

In many spiritual traditions it is common to regard darkness and the unknown as sacred and the source of a spiritual life. Often the divine guardians and guides of the deep, of the dark, are goddesses. Parmenides' teacher in his journey to the underworld is a goddess. This is not to say that the underworld or dark is feminine, which trivializes the teachings into a gender psychology. There are both gods and goddesses associated with all the worlds and dimensions of being. Rather, this association represents the parenting principles of spiritual guidance. We are mothered and fathered in the journey by being given nourishment, encouragement, consequences to our actions, lessons, unconditional love, and a flow of life energy. To go on the journey is to return home to our source and our original nature, to the divine parents from whom all existence arises and all life is sustained.

I mention goddesses here because in my experience during retreats the imagery that arose was often of a goddess, not only a god. In so much of Western culture, the male image of gods has been so prevalent that the goddess is often overlooked. This neglect has led to a kind of politics about the relative power and importance of "The Goddess" and "God." My experience suggests that the qualities of a god are in each goddess and the qualities of the goddess are in each god. Gender projections onto these profound and power energies are misleading and cut us off from their true nature.

In their book *Twilight Goddess,* Thomas Cleary and Sartaz Aziz explain how in Buddhist mythology, goddesses appear "primarily not as bestowers of boons but as teachers, guides, or helpers on the spiritual path."[10] What is of particular interest here is their discussion of the goddesses who act as guides and protectors of the teaching in the great sutra, the Flower Ornament Scripture. Each goddess represents a wisdom quality and gives the story's pilgrim a teaching and transmission. Most of these goddesses are designated as "night goddess." "Nighttime means darkness, and in darkness is invisibility and unknowing. All these images are related symbolically in referring to mystical experience."[11] Each night goddess is a source of light—the light of truth, transcendental insight, and joyous eyes that illuminate the world—to name a few. These night goddesses encircle the enlightenment site of Vairocana, the Illuminator, who represents primal awareness.

In this teaching there are also day goddesses, and part of the point is that both day and night have critical roles in the journey to profound wisdom. It is not a matter of embracing one and rejecting the other; this would contradict the very essence of the teachings. We want to engage and grow from both.

4 Retreats in Darkness in Other Traditions

The ground of the soul is dark.

—Meister Eckhart

Practitioners in all the traditions, including those from the ancient schools in the west, used many techniques to achieve clarity and open to the gifts of the gods. They would use meditations, incantations, breath control, prayers, and dream practices. All of these were designed to loosen the hold of ordinary senses and everyday habits, creating access to the dimensions of awareness that are beyond time and space and beyond concepts and mundane knowledge.

One of the settings for doing these practices was the cave. There are many stories of wisdom seekers, prophets, temple initiates, yogis, and mystics spending extended periods in caves where they received visions, trained their minds, and contacted the divine.

In the Taoist tradition dark caves have been used for thousands of years for inner alchemy practices. In Taoism there is a saying, "When you go into the dark and this becomes total, the darkness soon turns into light." I was told by a friend who plays sitar that in India the tradition of musicians doing a *chilla*, an extended retreat for practice and prayer, was sometimes done in total darkness.

Many of the prophets of ancient Israel and Greece would retreat to caves or dark places to receive divine wisdom. Prophecy in those days was not primarily about telling the future. It involved giving voice to what is beyond the ordinary, being a spokesperson for the divine. A prophet was someone who was able to enter another state of consciousness, had the capacity to receive the wisdom and energy of the sacred without being overwhelmed, and could then articulate and transmit the insights and wisdom from that dimension into the sensory world of other people.

Ancient Greek Practitioners: Parmenides and Pythagoras

Peter Kingsley, in his book *In the Dark Places of Wisdom*, argues that Western civilization is rooted in the mystical and philosophical tradition of Parmenides and Pythagoras. Their mysticism was grounded in their connection to gods and goddesses, in their practices of clarity and profound wisdom, and in their use of "incubation in darkness." These fathers of philosophy laid the foundations for what we now know as geometry, physics, astronomy, chemistry, rhetoric, and logic. Their practicality as well as their connection to the sacred derived from a deep understanding of the world and life based in profound wisdom.

For the ancient Greeks, particularly those who settled in what is now southern Italy, these people were called "the wise" because they were carriers and transmitters of the divine, were able to perceive beyond and behind appearances, and were able to use and interpret dreams, oracles, and the paradoxical nature of life.

Parmenides, whom Kingsley places as the father of Western philosophy, wrote a poem that describes his journey into the darkness of the underworld, how he got there, the wisdom teachings he received from the goddess, and her description of the deceptions of the world we ordinarily live in.

Like sacred initiation in cultures all over the world, initiates in pre-Socratic Greece sought to forge their own links to the divine. The initiation was a bridge to the sacred world where each initiate connected to a family of gods, establishing a home in that divine domain. They then lived in two worlds and were prepared before death to transition from their material homes to their home in the other world.

Parmenides uses the language of poetry and myth because metaphor is the only way we can point to the multidimensional meanings of experience and wisdom that are lost in concepts and literalism. The journey is a metaphor not simply for an idea, but for the actual practices and steps necessary to find clarity and wisdom, and to achieve a working relationship with the divine. His writing describes his experiences in the dark caves below the temples of Apollo and his working with death and the impermanent nature of reality to grow as a healer, priest, and teacher.

Parmenides writes:

> The mares that carry me as far as longing can reach rode on, once they had come and fetched me onto the legendary road of the divinity that carries the man who knows through the vast and dark unknown. And on I was carried as the mares, aware just where to go, kept carrying me straining at the chariot; and young women led the way. And the axle in the hubs let out the sound of a pipe blazing from the pressure of the two well-rounded wheels at either side, as they rapidly led on: young women, girls, daughters of the Sun who had left the mansions of Night for the light and pushed back the veils from their faces with their hands.
>
> There are the gates of the pathways of Night and Day,

held fast in place between the lintel above and a threshold of stone; and they reach up into the heavens, filled with gigantic doors. And the keys—that now open, now lock—are held fast by Justice: she who always demands exact returns. And with soft seductive words the girls cunningly persuaded her to push back immediately, just for them, the bar that bolts the gates. And as the doors flew open, making the bronze axles with their pegs and nails spin—now one, now the other in their pipes, they created a gaping chasm. Straight through and on the girls held fast their course for the chariot and horses, straight down the road.

And the goddess welcomed me kindly, and took my right hand in hers and spoke these words as she addressed me: "Welcome young man, partnered by immortal charioteers, reaching our home with the mares that carry you. For it was no hard fate that sent you travelling this road—so far away from the beaten track of humans—but Rightness, and Justice. And what's needed is for you to learn all things: both the unshaken heart of persuasive Truth and the opinions of mortals, in which there's nothing that can truthfully be trusted at all. But even so, this too you will learn—how beliefs based on appearance ought to be believable as they travel all through all there is."[12]

Kingsley points out that for Parmenides, night and darkness represent the domain of ignorance. To be ignorant of something is to ignore it. Thus it remains unknown. The world of the sacred tends to be ignored in ordinary life with its narrow concerns and fear of death. It is precisely in this unknown realm where the seeds of wisdom reside. Any authentic wisdom path must travel through this world that is ignored when our attention is captured by everyday material and emotional preoccupations.

According to Parmenides, we are carried on the journey by divine forces, not by willpower or effort, although these may be important to start. Once we have prepared, we give ourselves over and are taken straight to where we need to go. At the same time, it is the strength of longing, a deep passion or desire, that determines how far we can go. "The longing is what turns us inside out until we find the sun and the moon and stars inside."[13]

Being in touch with our deepest longings and working with them, rather than fleeing from them or trying to appease them, is one of the tasks in spiritual work. Our longing is so deep and vast that nothing that we consume—food, things, relationships, or experiences—can ever contain it or satisfy it. Even temporary satisfaction of small desires never lasts, and only serves to keep us haunted by the sense that there is something more.

Sometimes this haunting appears as sadness, discouraging us from everything we think of wanting. Our reaction is to run from this pain and grief and fight it with anger and/or withdrawal. It may even feel insane as we experience the hollowness when we ignore our own deepest voices calling us. The problem is not the sadness; it is the running from the sadness and the fear of inquiring, deeper into the dark unknown of our own souls.

In his journey to the underworld, Parmenides is guided by the daughters of the Sun. This is because the home of the Sun is the underworld, the world of darkness. The Sun belongs in the underworld; that is the place it arises from and returns to. The source of light, including both the material light of the Sun and the Clear Light of divine insight, has its home in darkness.

If this seems paradoxical, it is. In darkness, endless space can accommodate and include all contradictions, making a home for paradox. To the Pythagoreans of ancient Greece and the teachers in Eastern traditions, the sun, the moon, and the stars were reflections or creations of the invisible light of the heart, or the ultimate nature of all being. This was often characterized as an underworld because there was the realization that we cannot ascend without going down to the depths. We cannot comprehend the vastness of the outer expanse without knowing the boundless nature of the inner expanse.

This journey to the world of darkness was often seen as confronting the fire of the underworld that has the power to purify and transform us. Everything, light and dark, is part of the process of growth and there are no shortcuts. Everything has to be included. To find true clarity means facing utter darkness.

As Kingsley describes the journey of Parmenides, "to reach there, where every direction is available and everything merges with its opposite, you have to go down into the darkness—into the world of death where Night and Day both come from."[14]

Kingsley carefully makes a case that the ancient Greeks had the practice of retreating to places in the earth, often below temples of Apollo, the sun god. There healers and priests would "incubate" in darkness and do nothing. The practitioner would surrender and wait for healing or wisdom to come "from another level of awareness and another level of being."[15]

In many parts of ancient Greece, Apollo was a many-faceted god of healing, of incubation, and of the sun. This multidimensional divinity was also intimately associated with night, darkness, caves, the underworld, and death.

According to Kingsley, this is "why, at the Anatolian town of Hierapolis, Apollo's temple was right above the cave descending down to the underworld. And it's why at other famous oracle centres in Anatolia his temples were built just the same way—above a cave giving access to the underworld that was entered by his priest and by initiates at the dead of night."[16]

Kingsley describes how Pythagoras incorporated the ancient Greek techniques of incubation and descent.

As a sign of how dedicated he was to the goddesses of the

underworld he made his new home in southern Italy into a temple: built a special underground room where he'd go and stay motionless for long periods of time. Afterwards he'd describe how he had gone down to the underworld and come back as a messenger from the gods.

The reports about him say he taught his closest disciples to do the same thing, and the language of the reports shows it was the practice of incubation that he taught them. The mysteries of the underworld remained central for later Pythagoreanism—and so did the role that Pythagoreans kept giving to incubation. For this wasn't a tradition of people who were fond of ideas and beautiful theories. They were people who knew how to die before they died.[17]

Part II
A Western Practitioner
in Dark Retreat

> This word is a hidden word
> and comes in the darkness of the night.
> To enter this darkness put away
> all voices and sounds
> all images and likenesses.
>
> —Meister Eckhart

This section is a mix of journal selections, explanations, and teachings from my month-long retreat in 1998. By sharing my journals, I intend to provide you with descriptions of the experiential basis for this book and to give a less conceptual, more personal way for you to relate to the profound teachings surrounding spiritual work in general, and dark retreat in particular. Parts 3 and 4 will present a more detailed discussion of the philosophy of this work from both Western and Tibetan points of view.

1 Setting Up My Retreat

My Goals and Aspirations for Doing Dark Retreat

My primary goal in deciding to do dark retreats was to accelerate and deepen my own practice. I did not approach retreats because they were required or because they were the spiritually fashionable thing to do. In fact, few people I had known had done any kind of dark retreat.

I had done enough solitary retreats to know the value they held, and the openness, stability, peace, and joy that were the fruits of meditating in retreat. My instinct told me that after more than two decades of practice, darkness might hold some treasures, and that the innate, luminous nature of the mind would become more evident.

My initial dark retreats confirmed those hopes and held out the prospect of even further realization of my own wisdom nature and deeper connection with the source of all being, with God. I also wanted to do additional work with my reactive habits, core fears, and needy addictions that continued to play a role in my everyday life.

Wisdom is hidden in the soul realm of the unknown, which is often equated with death. In all the great traditions, facing death and the unknown, something most of us avoid, is the price we must pay for sacred wisdom. The journey to the unknown of the divine takes us out of life as we know it and often straight towards what we fear.

In a dark retreat, there are no people there. Little is familiar, for even the few objects we are used to are sensed in a new way without sight. We enter a world of the unknown that is generally ignored in our everyday lives. We need to be willing to die to our life of habits and enter a dark and strange place. We die before we die, no longer living on the surface ourselves.

Prior to my first retreats, I had trepidation about what might happen in the dark. As a young child, the fear of aliens coming into my bedroom at night had haunted me. The traces of that fear probably lingered in some form.

I had both anticipation and discomfort, which are common, when I decide to explore and experience something unknown. I sensed that I might be exposing my innermost self to the possibility of being ripped apart in the isolation and intensity of the retreat. I was determined to take what in mythology is called a hero's journey, without the idea of becoming a hero. My hope was to open sufficiently so that wisdom would destroy my reactive habits and identities.

Shock Points

Retreats like this set up the conditions that allow our spiritual growth to progress beyond its current capacity. We reach certain critical points in our development. At those points we are challenged to go beyond where we are and all that we have been, to becoming new again. We open to being worked by the situation and by forces that seem beyond our comprehension. The impact of these forces was called a "shock" by George Gurdjieff and he considered it important to our development through the points in what he called our "octave of being."

Shock points provide an extra measure of energetic juice in our growth. The experience is metaphorically like being struck by lightning. We are not the same person afterwards. There are shock points which arise out of everyday life if we are ready, there are those induced by a teacher, and there are those which arise out of the conditions of our practice.

When we successfully work with a shock point, we experience a new way of perceiving the world and a different foundation for being and doing. We experience a discontinuity between what came before and what is now. It is like being born again in a new way. I was reminded of the shock points I had experienced in the past.

Witnessing my son Micah's birth over thirty years ago was a powerful shock point, revealing the miracle of life, the sense of living presence and divine energy. As he entered the material world to become independent of the womb, I entered the world of wonder, delight, and love.

Over the course of more than thirty years of dedicated meditation, I have felt my world become shaky and dissolve in meetings with spiritual teachers. I received a shock when I received an empowerment and blessing by the Karmapa, the head of the Karma Kagyu lineage in Tibetan Buddhism. I remember the sense of light and bliss that seemed to fill the room and vibrate throughout my body. A similar experience occurred when I first saw His Holiness Dilgo Khyentse Rinpoche, another great spiritual master and teacher of mine.

My inner being was similarly affected in two other meetings with spiritual teachers—receiving teachings from Chögyam Trungpa Rinpoche beginning in 1971, and encountering Lar Short for the first time in 1985. In the midst of the confusion that followed each event, I experienced my heart opening.

Ordinary life is filled with shocks as well. Besides witnessing Micah's birth, another was when my first wife and I decided to get divorced more than twenty-five years ago. This challenged all my images

23

of how things were supposed to work out and raised a bundle of emotional and psychological issues. My meditation practice initially was distracted and highly charged, with my mind being swept away at the drop of a thought. Gradually, as I persevered, a special relaxation set in and a clarity became evident.

A year later when I felt that my meditation had served me well as a kind of crutch through a difficult time and I wanted to find out what changes had really emerged in my core way of being, I made a conscious decision to tap my more outrageous potentials. I had little idea what that would entail or what would evoke the wild side of me.

Shortly after making this decision, I stopped meditating and got involved in a wildly romantic relationship with someone who was a number of years younger than I and whose emotions were like a roller coaster. The wild ride of that relationship challenged me to the core. I felt insecurities and distrust that I had not known since adolescence. I became periodically obsessive about my love and the relationship. As I lived with this situation, I returned to meditating with a new perspective and with the clear desire to work with the emotional energies that were sweeping through me like tidal waves. As my sitting practice became established again, I concentrated some of my attention on being mindful and some on containing and balancing the energy of my feelings. Over time I became increasingly grounded in an open way of being and in a sense of hosting.

During this period another shock point occurred during a retreat at Karma Choling in Vermont. We were sitting 12 to 14 hours a day, with breaks only for meals and chores. I remember sitting with the question of "How do I get beyond my own identity and my own observer?" It was more than a question. It was an agenda, a goal. I would sit there watching myself sit and think. Then I would observe myself watching myself thinking. Then I would observe myself observing myself watching myself thinking. And so on. It seemed as though I was standing between two mirrors seeing the infinite regression of images being reflected and hoping that there would be a point where the image of me would disappear. I kept wondering how to get to this thing called "no self," beyond ego or no identity. I would keep trying to get beyond watching without success, and would go back to my breath and then back into my inquiry.

The longer I sat with this, the more desperate I became. At one point I sat on my cushion, maintaining my upright, dignified posture with my aching back and sore knees, and tears were pouring out from my eyes. I wept quietly off and on for hours, feeling the despair, and yet determined to continue asking for help. I was not even sure what or whom I asked for help from. I simply knew that I could not do this myself and appealed to forces beyond me to work with me. I reached a point where something in me kept trying, and at the same time surrendered. Eventually I relaxed, whether out of exhaustion or simply hitting the limit of that pattern of thoughts and feelings. Without my noticing it, I was simply sitting, openly, peacefully, mindfully, alert, awake, and energetic. It was close to an hour before I noticed that the issue of self-consciousness and the despair had dissolved and I was simply abiding in a sense of being and presence. From that time on, more than twenty years ago, the shift in my ground of being has remained. Issues like boredom and getting out of myself no longer arise.

By the time I began to do dark retreats, my practice was stable and I had been teaching meditation for many years. While I had experienced visions, received unknown teachings, had periods of continuous consciousness, received transmission of profound energies, and been empowered to teach others, I was acutely aware of my shortcomings and the subtle gaps in my sense of belonging in and to the world, life, and all being. I admired and aspired to the accomplishments and splendor of great masters, and to the powerful wisdom presence of many of my teachers. I still felt awkward in my relationship to the sacred, wondering if the sacred richness that friends and teachers like Tenzin Wangyal and Martín Prechtel experienced in the world would ever be the ground I walked on, lived in, and taught from.

In the spiritual search we often try to learn from teachers and others who seem to have profound knowledge. This can be useful as long as we do not settle into the safety of believing the word of others. By making the decision to do a dark retreat, we are taking the risk of searching inside ourselves and in the darkness all around us for the wisdom that we can embody.

Years of hanging out with wonderful poets, musicians, spiritual teachers, and artists, all of whom conveyed an authentic sense of the richly profound nature of life, had made me realize the shallowness of my early attempts to ascend into a simple higher consciousness. I noticed that when we seek the divine or happiness only in the heavens, we lose our depth and create a barrier of fear and struggle between spiritual realization and the fullness of life in all its pleasing and unpleasing forms. It is impossible to reach the true clarity of awareness by rejecting the darkness, the power and richness of the earth, and the need to include everything.

In my initial dark retreats, I realized that it is so much more difficult to see and know the inner lights in the midst of external light. I understood that very important insights, wisdom, and experience are the treasures awaiting me in the dark. After my first three-day dark retreat, I got enough understanding to know that to mine this gold, it was not enough to dig at the topsoil of my thoughts and emotions. I needed to go more deeply into the darkness to what lay beyond the feelings, thoughts, and visions, to the source of my very consciousness and sense of being.

In the solitude of the dark retreat, I confronted demons and grief that I did not know I had or that I thought I had worked through in other retreats. I knew enough to realize that the experience was not about feeling good, although I was open to that. Facing all the contradictions, ambiguities, and pain was essential to reaching the unconditional, intangible fortune that was the promise of this work, however remote it seemed.

A major goal of a spiritual journey (some see it as the only true goal) is discovering or recognizing the place where all things converge, all opposites meet, where upper contains lower and lower contains upper, inner and outer are boundless, day and night both have their home, and heaven and earth have their source.

During the first week of my month-long retreat in 1998 I wrote some of my intentions for this journey into darkness.

1. To encounter and open UP to unknown
2. To challenge my fears
3. To discover and be transformed by (at the personal level) true nature, natural mind, Essence, the Divine, Ein Sof, Allah, The Great Mother
4. To train my heart, mind, and body to better serve those I love, friends, my students, my teachers, the world, nature, and life
5. To celebrate the little blessings of living which I attend to more in the dark
6. To gather all my flaws in celebration
7. To dissolve completely

Another way of putting some of this: to meet myself in each moment of life, in every object, in every detail. Or rather, to meet the world and life through being met. To meet myself through being met.

I always wanted to be able to use all experience, all activities, all emotions as gateways to the sacred and as food for my growth. I also wanted to be able to create beauty and be of service to my family, friends, community, and the world. I wanted to craft a life of beauty and wisdom, to offer not only to the world as a legacy, but also to the divine forces that have so generously given and nourished life. I wanted to deepen my connection to the larger stories and worlds that I am a part of, and to become a conscious contributor to these stories and worlds.

When I was introduced to dark retreats by Tenzin Wangyal, he held out no promises or visions. He simply suggested that it would be a good thing to do and see what happened. He gave only minimal instructions and goals, emphasizing that initially one should simply relax and become familiar with the experience. Over the years he has continued his support as I have incorporated more advanced practices.

Preparations

When doing a dark retreat, the inner preparation involves both teachings and practices that open our attention and release what we think we know. We want to become so versed in the teachings that we do not think about them, shifting our attention to what is beyond.

I usually begin more intensive practice about a week before doing a significant retreat, reviewing instructions that will be incorporated into the retreat practices. For the first dark retreats I received instructions from Tenzin Wangyal beforehand. Since he was not in the area during the retreat, he would check in with me by phone (he would call and my wife would bring me the phone). His suggestions were helpful and the encouragement, connection, and support were powerfully inspiring, energizing, and satisfying. During the time of the 1998 retreat, the primary focus of this book, Tenzin was out of the country. We connected before and after the retreat. I had also received some instructions and encouragement from Lopon Tenzin Namdak when I had seen him at a previous summer retreat during one of his visits to the United States.

When my students do dark retreats (varying in length from two days to two weeks), I check in with them and give them guidance every day or every other day. This allows me to gauge how they are progressing, help with any problems they may be having, and suggest practices based on their experiences. They have reported that this regular contact and instruction are helpful. If they are doing retreats elsewhere, we use the telephone to keep in touch. I will call and their caretaker will then connect them.

Our mindsets and attitudes upon entering the retreat can set the stage for our experiences in the retreat. It would be great to enter with a sense of clarity, openness, joy, and resting in our true nature, but this is more the fruit of the retreat than a prerequisite. Some of the attitudes I have found useful are looking forward to a wonderful rest and vacation from the pressures of everyday life; curiosity about what will arise; longing to get the clarity, wisdom, and the fruits of the practices and the retreat; dedication to growth; treating whatever arises as an opportunity to learn; connection to the teachers and the teachings; sense of support from the community; service to the larger community and the world, and wanting to be a beneficial presence; confidence from the fact that others have successfully navigated through such retreats for thousands of years and brought back treasures from their efforts; and gratitude for this opportunity to learn, grow, and create benefit and beauty for ourselves, others, and the world.

There is also one other important quality that we want to have in our journeys—a sense of humor. Taking ourselves very seriously creates enormous barriers to relaxing into our nature and opening to the unknown. For example, in an early retreat I found myself intently looking for signs and visions that I had heard about. Then I looked at my situation and said to myself, "Waiting for the mind to self-liberate is like watching grass grow."

Some of the practical preparations included the following:

1. Making sure the retreat space was light-tight. This required spending 30 to 40 minutes in the room in the dark before the retreat. It takes about that amount of time for the eyes to adjust and your perception to become sensitive enough to detect even the faintest leaks of light from the outside.

2. Bringing in the clothes and snacks you would need for the period. I created a way of laying out the different items so I could easily determine what I was selecting. This was also true of medications and vitamins. Creating and remembering the organization of my things made everyday functioning much easier.

3. I had an electric kettle for heating water and a small refrigerator (without a light) in the bathroom of the retreat space. Since it was winter and my respiratory sensitivities react to the dryness of the heaters, I also had a humidifier in the retreat room. I used black electrical tape to cover the lighted indicators on the machine.

4. My wife, friends, and members of the Dedicated Life community brought me meals and helped with other needs as they arose. In general they brought two meals a day, breakfast and dinner. Lunches I prepared on my own from dehydrated soups and food I kept in the small refrigerator. There were a number of days that I also handled my own breakfast, particularly when my wife, Karen, was away during the last week of the retreat. Involving other people in the retreat was a way of sharing the retreat and deepening the bonds within the community.

5. Of course, one of the critical matters is taking care of business before entering the retreat. For those of us who do not live in monasteries, who have family and work obligations, and have many responsibilities that are not generally shared, this can be challenging. Sometimes things come up during the retreat that require immediate attention. For example, during one of my retreats, my youngest son and his wife needed to know some financial information from me in order to make an offer on buying a house. This could not wait until the retreat was completed, so I briefly spoke with him by phone without leaving the retreat. It is often more problematic to not deal with important matters that might haunt your thinking. Handling such urgent items without leaving the dark can be the most appropriate solution for others and less distracting for the practitioner.

Practices

My practices during the retreat included basic mindfulness practice, many traditional Buddhist and Bön practices, dream and sleep practices, various yogas and chi kungs, writing meditations, inquiries, and compassion meditations. Some of the practices are described or referred to in the text of my journals from the 1998 retreat. Others can be found in appendix A. It should also be understood that many of the practices that I worked with were introduced to me by my teachers and are meant to be shared only in the intimate context of a teacher-student relationship. If you are interested, it would be worthwhile to find a qualified teacher to assess your needs and give you appropriate teachings.

In general I did four to six meditation sessions a day. The periods would be in the early morning before breakfast, the middle and late morning, the early and late afternoon, and an evening session after dinner. The length of time of each increased over the course of the retreat as my stamina grew. Early in the retreat, each session might be an hour to an hour and a half. By the end of the first week, many sessions probably ran for three hours or more, particularly those in the morning and afternoon.

At the beginning of each session, I would honor the teachings and my teachers, and invoke their support for my meditation. As I reflected on my teachers and the great wise people and practitioners that have inspired me, my invocations were ways to maintain a correct relationship with the wisdom energies these people embody and to empower those energies in the present, experiencing and using the living presence of these great beings.

During this month-long retreat I decided to do twenty-four days of practices related to the realms of suffering and the *Dhyani* Buddhas, who are the meditation Buddhas, the aspects of awakened wisdom consciousness. These practices are called the Heart of Compassion sadhana (referred to as HOC in my journals) that I have practiced in various forms for more than twenty years. Discussion of many of the teachings relating to this practice can be found in the book I wrote with Lar Short, *Opening the Heart of Compassion: Transform Suffering through Buddhist Psychology and Practice*. The sadhana is derived from teachings in the Nyingma lineage of Tibetan Buddhism and is similar to the dark retreat practices of the *Dzogchen yangtse klongchen.*

My practice involves meditating on each of the six realms of suffering and purifying their fundamental confusion to reveal their wisdom nature that arises as a Dhyani Buddha. Part of the practice is *tsa lung,* or the yoga of the subtle channels (*tsa*), the subtle energies (*lung*), and the bindus (*thigle*). Tsa lung works with breathing practices, visualizations, yoga positions, movements, and in this case sound, to release our contracted awareness into the subtle wisdom qualities of consciousness. In the darkness it is much easier to see the radiant colors of each of the wisdom qualities and to experience abiding in a Buddha field.

The sadhana also involves *tonglen* practice of receiving the suffering of others and sending the wisdom energies from the heart center to others. This is a practice with many dimensions and profound effects. Through tonglen we open our hearts, sense our connection to all life, including all the painful conditions in the world, and share all that is wholesome, good, and wise with all other beings, with the desire that these qualities spread and are experienced by everyone.

I called on protector deities, particularly the Bön deity of Yeshe Walmo, when ending meditations sessions. This practice sets up a part of my mind to notice when I am getting distracted, agitated, or reactive and reminds me to be consciously present.

I closed each session with a dedication of the benefits of the practice. We do not simply work for ourselves, making the value dependent on our situations and memories. In dedicating the merits of our work to others, we transmit the qualities and energies that result from practice into the world so that others can receive them and carry on the value. This amplifies the effect and keeps the work alive.

The dedication shifts attention to the world around us, integrating the external with our internal practice. The sights, sounds, and events that occur then become stimuli for extending our conscious work beyond formal practice. In the relaxed space of meditating in the dark, everything that arises becomes a reminder of openness and the desire to remain alert and present. Everything becomes a support for practice. All sounds are the voice of wisdom. All visions are the expressions of clarity, and all sensations are the caress of presence.

At the beginning of the retreat there was the sense that what arose was created by my own mind. Over time I also had the sense that the clarity, insights, and wisdom were gifts of some greater force that I had opened to. The same was true of dreams. Some dreams were obviously the processing of my personal experience. Others seemed to be communications or gifts from Grace.

Dreaming and Dream Practices

Last Night as I Was Sleeping

Last night, as I was sleeping,
I dreamt—marvelous error!—
that a spring was breaking
out in my heart.
I said: Along which secret aqueduct,
Oh water, are you coming to me,
water of a new life
that I have never drunk?

Last night, as I was sleeping,
I dreamt—marvelous error!—
that I had a beehive
here inside my heart.
And the golden bees
were making white combs
and sweet honey
from my old failures.

Last night, as I was sleeping,
I dreamt—marvelous error!—
that a fiery sun was giving
light inside my heart.
It was fiery because I felt
warmth as from a hearth,
and sun because it gave light
and brought tears to my eyes.

Last night, as I was sleeping,
I dreamt—marvelous error!—
that it was God I had
here inside my heart.[18]

—Antonio Machado
(translated by Robert Bly)

The significance of dreams in spiritual work has been recognized by all the great traditions since humans began formulating teachings on the sacred. The prophets of ancient Israel; the healers and oracles of Greece; the aboriginal peoples of Australia; native Pacific islanders; Jesus; Mohammed; the Hindu, Taoist, and Buddhist masters; and shamans from all over the world all utilized the special powers of dream in their relationship to the sacred and in their cultivation of sacred awareness and spiritual capacity.

Dreams are both real and unreal, like everything in life. They have personal qualities and aspects that are collective and transpersonal. Dreams are all reflections of ourselves. Some dreams process the events, thoughts, and experiences of daily life; others are characterized by alertness and consciousness of dreaming while it is occurring; still others give us visions of Clear Light, blessings, profound teachings, sacred signs, and energetic transmissions.

In dreams, time and space are fluid and malleable. Reality is flexible and more clearly insubstantial, giving us insight into the nature of all projections of the mind. Dreams can introduce us to other worlds and dimensions of being. They give us experiences of our consciousness freed from the constraints of a physical body, and thus glimpses of what lies beyond death.

Dreams have been used for healing, for clairvoyance, and for spiritual awakening. Shamans and healers throughout history have entered dream states to diagnose ailments and to receive treatment instructions, and have induced specific dreamstates in patients to correct imbalances and repair the tears in their worlds to make them whole again.

Oracles are people who use dream states to contact the gods and make divinations about the likely course of events. They also receive guidance about how to navigate the challenges that are on the horizon.

There are also teachings and texts which relate and explain the incorporation of dreams in the cultivation of clarity, freedom, mobilization of our innate psychic capacities, and continuous conscious awareness. In the Chinese wisdom stories, the philosopher Chuang Tzu dreamed he was a butterfly. Upon awakening, he wondered whether he was a man dreaming of being a butterfly or a butterfly dreaming he was a man.

The Tibetan dream and sleep practices teach us how to awaken within the dream and to practice spiritually while sleeping. In these practices we learn that dreams can be altered by our attention and decisions, that they are like mirages, that our daily waking perceptions are also mirages, that all life is impermanent and cannot be grasped, and that conscious dreamwork can lead us to a profound sense of wholeness, harmony, and unity. As Tenzin Wangyal points out in his book *The Tibetan Yogas of Dream and Sleep,* "the goal of dream practice is liberation; our intent should be to realize what is beyond dreams altogether."[19]

2 Taking the Plunge: Opening the Retreat

Day 1

Lots of matters to complete before beginning the retreat.

Reviewed teachings from Bön tradition.

As I slow down, I am coming home again to dark retreat. I have a home in here already even though it is a new room which I had built specifically as a retreat room. I can still smell the fresh paint.

Deep gratitude.

Ritual opening of the retreat with blessings, bows to the directions, invoking the wisdom energies of the teachings, of my teachers, of all wisdom beings, of my spiritual communities and community of family and friends, of nature, and of the divine, gratitude for this wonderful opportunity, dedication of my effort for the benefit of the DLI community, others, and the world.

Am starting, having stayed up all night . . . to prepare the retreat space and move my things in for the month.

Being in the dark meant that I had to discover the world in an entirely new way. The encounter with the blackness, with the feel and texture of everything, with reliance on memory and position, led to and even required new approaches to daily living—not simply routines in which to operate, but rituals that would bring a sense of the sacred to the process, that would express my sense of awe at the miracle of imagination, memory, support, of all that I got to experience.

The activities prior to turning out the lights resemble those when we are about to depart on a vacation—checking all the items I would need for a month, making arrangements with my office, my clients, and Institute business, and saying "see you in a month" to family, friends, and associates. In the case of a dark retreat, there are the added tasks of reviewing any written teachings and practices that are going to be used in the retreat which are not part of my regular routine and of looking carefully around the room to make a mental picture of where everything is. This picture is a map that will guide my movements and blind searches during the coming days and weeks.

As in any retreat, it is important to begin with a ritual that requests the blessings of the space and all the unseen forces (invisible in the light as well as the dark) that can influence the course of the retreat. The ritual also provided a transition from the light of everyday life to the space of my new home and redirected my attention to the purposes and requirements of the retreat. The consecration of the place and the activities set up the environment both externally and internally for an effective practice and profound experience. It also reaffirmed my connection to other people and the larger story that my life and work are a part of.

Mornings in particular were times of ritual. The sense of renewal and possibilities as I would awaken into each new day was clearer and stronger than on the outside. That sense is only fleetingly noticed and usually ignored as we get on with the regular multitude of tasks for the day. After a while we may not even notice, or we may awaken with a sense of being overwhelmed, of dread, programmed into our habit bodies by days, months, and years of rush.

Night provides the most compatible time to begin a retreat, coinciding with the natural rhythms of the body and mind. In this retreat, there was so much preparation that it was late at night when I shut out the light, and probably morning by the time I completed my opening rituals and meditations. There was no hurry, no schedule to fit into, and no reason to worry about sleep since I would have plenty of time to get whatever sleep I needed.

Much of the first couple of days was spent sleeping and recovering from sleep deprivation. Most of us who are busy working, playing, having relationships, and participating in many activities do not get enough sleep on a regular basis.

I have thought for some time that the sleep deficit most people live with is partly responsible for overeating, excessive activity, loss of patience, a tendency to emotional swings or numbness, and an appetite for passive entertainment such as television. In our stuporous everyday state, we become addicts of stimulation.

Day 2

Feeling more settled.

Sleeping a lot.

Had repeated dream of waking up feeling parched and drinking water. Then I realize that I am still asleep.

I am loving the space and very happy with my design.

Practiced today for some of the meditations facing east. Some facing west.

Such a blessing.

Had another dream. This involved a woman artist showing a frontal picture of a nude woman with one area near the crotch left blank except for a number. She demonstrates the position in the picture, points to her thigh, which is also blank of color, and says "painting by numbers." I wonder if I am supposed to fill in the blank in her and if this is dreaming by numbers. I have realized that I am dreaming and open my eyes in the dark to see the dream continue in the totally black dark retreat room. I see the dream unfolding clear as daylight. The image became rose-tinted and evolved into cubist images and gradually dissolved into a Clear Light.

Still settling.

Some practices and aspects of the experience seem to pick up from the end of last year's three-week retreat.

Feel even more at home.

Thoughts, feelings, and images that arise dissolve very quickly into a quiet clear presence.

I feel my heart opening and my chest expanding.

Even in this dark, still, silent place, I sense a vibrant, pulsing, alive universe—not of this room but of the world.

The dark is completely intimate and close, and vast, without ending. It is in my face and gives me the freedom of infinite space. It holds me close and releases me into boundlessness.

Rainbows have begun to appear—rather, rainbow lights.

I see them, then they dissolve into a kind of Clear Light and then they reappear.

They tend to appear directly in front of me.

I am still too tired to do as much practice as I would like, and I continue to think about work, my writing, Mom, Karen, my children, etc.

At the beginning of each day I did some exercises. During the first days of this retreat and for all of the days of my first couple of retreats, I would confine my physical activity to stretching. One of the purposes of a retreat is to let everything relax and to allow the energies of the body-mind to settle so that a natural way of being, clarity, and calmness emerge. We begin like a glass of muddy water. By letting everything become still, the dirt and particles that cloud and color the water gradually settle to the bottom and the water reveals its true nature, becoming clear. Vigorous exercise can excite the energies of the body and agitate the flow of thoughts and feelings. Rapid and extensive activity can make it more difficult to sit quietly and remain alert.

Once clarity is somewhat stable, then the movements are experienced as occurring within the natural stillness of the mind and of the space.

As we begin any retreat, the conscious work of doing the retreat confronts our old habits. For me this showed up in my first short retreat. I remember preparing to do some stretching by putting on my exercise shorts when it occurred to me that they were unnecessary because not even I could see me.

When I relax in the dark, a familiar intimacy greets me. We are conceived in darkness, take form in the dark, and are born from darkness into light. Light itself arises from the dark. Darkness can evoke the sense of an original home.

I was again filled with the sense of wonder—at the stillness, at the way the blackness enfolds and surrounds me and seems to reach inside me, and at the way it extends my horizon out into infinite space.

Day 3

Longer meditations.

Began doing the Heart of Compassion Yoga and Sadhana.

Experienced the fragrances of wisdom energies.

Deep wish to be up to the service I am trying to do.

To live up to the blessing I have been given.

Often while abiding and listening deeply, I have a sense of being given a gift that is unknown, even to me. A secret gift that I must serve and that will reveal itself in its own time. I feel gifted by the earth, the heavens, by my teachers, by my family, friends, community and by the unknown (including unknown lineages of wisdom).

Writing in the Dark

Creating something of beauty from the experiences of the dark had become a practice of my retreats for a number of years. As I relax into my deepest nature, within a few days writing emerges naturally as a manifestation of the sacred space I have returned home to. For example, in the three-week dark retreat in 1997, on the fourth day I wrote this fragment of a poem:

mirror of darkness
reflecting the images of my mind
vast expanse in which to be lost and found
surrounds and caresses me and penetrates to my core
No fear in this black embrace
This womb, a primordial home
Free to relax and sing the body, the heart, and the mind.

During the third day of this retreat, I wrote a poem-like piece to express the sense and joy of being at home in the dark.

At home in the Dark

It is only in the dark that I am reminded of how blind I am in daily
        light.
It is through feeling water in the unseen space of my retreat room
that I am struck by the miracle of small things.
The song of the birds outside,
fragrance of cooked rice,
the mind releases its claim to the attention of the heart
so that I can open to what is.
With my heart's attention my being opens to and meets
each sound, smell, taste, and touch.
A flow of energy radiates
out in every step, touch, and act
as the world around me reveals its hidden nature
and I am exposed by it in all my nakedness.
Nothing is held beyond the moment.
Judgments and comments give way to presence.
Thundering silence and dynamic stillness
energize this meeting of the moment.
My heart celebrates this sacred posture of praise.

The praise echoes back as the celebration becomes mutual.
This eternal moment of resounding joy
simply serves the delicious glory
of the taste of cool fresh water in a dark home.

As I got into the retreat, writing notes, reflections, and journal entries flowed more readily and the habit took deeper root. Outside of retreats I do try to write, but am very inconsistent in my efforts at keeping a journal. The retreat writing would usually be done during an afternoon break in practices. Occasionally upon waking in the morning or from a short nap, I would write about the dreams or some inspiration that would come to me in lucid dreaming and sleeping.

The method I have developed for writing is quite simple. I use a thick pad of 5" x 8" paper. I place the index finger of my left hand on the left edge of the pad to mark where I begin a line. I write across the page and upon reaching the right edge, my left index finger moves down and I find it with my pen and begin another line. In reviewing my notes after the retreat, I found that I had written over or crossed lines only a handful of times in more than 200 pages of notes. Most pages only had a few sentences on them.

The poet Denise Levertov, who wrote in the dark about some of the visions that would come to her during the night, advised against bothering about "crossing your t's, dotting your i's." She cautioned to not "cover one word with the next" and to trust that one hand will instinctively assist the other "to keep each line clear of the next."[20]

Curiously, my handwriting during the first week or two was mostly straight across the page, normal sized, and similar to my regular writing. By the third week, the lines tended to arc downward and the writing got smaller.

At a later point in the retreat I noted that the writings could mislead anybody who might read the journals:

Day 19

It occurred to me that if someone were reading these notes, they would have a distorted impression of my retreat. I do not spend much time thinking and writing. The many hours spent on my cushion are characterized mostly as a calm, clear, abiding, filled with presence. My sittings will often run between two and three hours particularly in the mornings when my knees and back are fresh. There is rarely any drama going on; the effort is to stay open and relaxed with the center of my attention arising from my heart center and including my entire alive sense of being.

Most days, I was the only person in the house and, during times when Karen was traveling, there was often no one else there even at night. I found on Day 4 that I had still not released the background sense of responsibility for the house. As a parent listens for the variations in the sounds of sleep of a child, so a homeowner like me listens for the unusual sound in the house. The unconscious listening became apparent during the morning that day.

Day 4

After exercising I decided to check out the sound of a motor that appeared to have been left on and seemed constant. I put on slippers and my dark mask for my eyes which blocks all light. I mindfully made my way to the first floor to check out switches to the fans. Nothing was on that I could find by touch or sound. It may have been the sound of the furnace motor. As I blindly made my way through doors, around furniture, and unremembered objects, I was mindful of each step—paid absolute attention.

Later I realized how unconscious I was of my own agitation. Upon returning I settled into a profound, long meditation.

During the rest of this day, the practices were long, probably running about three hours for a session. During my practices with the Heart of Compassion, which works to transform the bodymind into a body of wisdom energy using conscious attention, physical movement, visualization, chanting, and abiding, rainbow lights would spread through the space, and fragrances filled the atmosphere. With each part of the practice, the colors would dissolve into Clear Light as I remained effortlessly, calmly abiding in an open clarity.

During break periods, I reflected on the importance of maintaining a sacred heart posture. The entire experience in retreat was sacred work. The aim, in contrast to the secular, material tone of our society, concerns living in a sacred world. This takes us beyond even bringing the sacred into life. In our culture we may need to begin by intentionally remembering the sacred and doing rituals, prayers, and meditations to have more balance. At the same time the greater goal involves placing the mental in service to sacred prayer and reflection, the emotional in service of sacred devotion, and our sense of being in the world as a sacred manifestation.

This sense of the sacred carried over into a dream I had that afternoon.

Dream:
Making way up a somewhat icy and snowy staircase.

Kick off snow to make it safer for kids.

Steep drop-off edge. Took off my fanny pack with wallet in it and used it to clear railing.

I approach the back door of an apartment. As I approach, the door swings open into the kitchen. A woman I know is there with many children and becomes a great mother. She says I can come in if I take off my shoes.

Once I am in, the scene changes. I am in a great chamber. A person appears in front of me. Gradually its face begins to transform. First the left eye goes blank, enlarges, and turns red. The mouth opens and fang-like teeth emerge at the edges. A huge third eye emerges at the center of the forehead. I recognize a fierce protector. Then I get the head to rotate. It has 3 faces. The second face is like a wild boar. The third face is totally peaceful, radiating compassion, joy, praise, and celebration. I felt blessed and held this being in my heart, and felt that I was mutually held in its heart.

During my practice after the dream, I decided to recall all my daily failings. I treated each as if it had a gift for me as I worked to make it a part of my sacred celebration of life. The "flaws" that I identified in this process included the following:

Pretension of being more together than I am.

Wanting to be a good example. This is both a flaw and a contribution. I want my presence to be beneficial, inspirational, and supportive of value.

Laziness.

Afraid somewhat of disappointing others. Try not to build expectations.

Want to impress.

Want to connect through achievements.

Ambitious.

Part of me wants fame.

Part wants the simplicity of being unknown.

Trap of periodically organizing financial picture.

Not wanting to show stupidity (heard of a sign that says, "Dare to be stupid").

Fear of asthma.

Wanting to look good, be healthy, and live a long time.

Get distracted when I need to write or get something finished.

Not writing letters.

Not knowing what to say.

Writing things that are not good English and that are small talk.

Occasionally wishing I lived alone, most of the time loving being married.

Not giving enough attention to my kids.

Not being generous enough.

Maintaining images.

Not giving thanks enough.

Not pushing students enough—not being demanding enough.
Fear of wasting my opportunity.

The process of recalling "flaws" reminded me of lines from a poem by David Whyte called "The Faces at Braga." He ends that poem with the following verses:

If only we could give ourselves
to the blows of the carver's hands,
the lines in our faces would be the trace lines of rivers

feeding the sea
where voices meet, praising the features
of the mountain and the cloud and the sky.

Our faces would fall away
until we, growing younger toward death
every day, would gather all our flaws in celebration

to merge with them perfectly,
impossibly, wedded to our essence,
full of silence from the carver's hands.[21]

3 Gradual Awakening

During the morning meditation on Day 5, the time of abiding in pure being included many experiences.

> In deep presence in addition to silence and stillness, I sometimes hear winds from an energetic dimension. Sometimes it sounds like the gentle surf of the ocean. At times I see the winds as currents of light, sometimes clear, sometimes colored. I also notice a fragrance, a little like some types of sweet and pungent incense.

When I simply hosted everything from a ground of pure being and presence, qualities of sound, light, and fragrances arose as if from another world. They were difficult to describe because they were not always the same as the sounds, colors, and odors I experience in my ordinary sensory life. They were not coming from some memory and then projected into the space of my retreat. They appeared to be aspects of the state of resting in my nature. They seemed to be natural manifestations of this state.

Images came to me in meditation and sleep practice. One looked like a pile of junk stacked high. As I continued to look at it, I could see a mandala. Like the shift in gaze of the "Magic Eye." This happened a couple of times and I realized that the ordinary contained a doorway and map to the sacred.

For purposes of doing meditations and yogas related to the six wisdom qualities and lights associated with the six realms of suffering, I divided most of the retreat into six periods of four days each. During the retreat I found that as I worked with each realm, my insights were both deepened and elaborated. I have been giving teachings on these topics for almost twenty years, and the practices still bring revelations, fresh understanding, and greater intensity to the sense of presence of each of the Dhyani Buddhas.

Day 5

Wisdom of possession—all objects, land, etc., are entrusted to us. It is up to each of us to invest them with our energy to bring them to life and bring out the sacred. It diminishes an object—a cup, a toothbrush, a knife—to be used unconsciously.

All objects should be used in service to the world.

Possession is a mutual process. The service and respect are both ways. When objects are not really seen and the possession is one way, they are dead or even demonic.

Each object is a messenger from the sacred. A reminder that we are part of a sacred world. (Not that the sacred is part of us.)

The world is meant to be shared as part of conscious community and celebration.

Day 6

Sense that the Wisdom of the animal realm is not only a sense of relating and interbeing, it is fully meeting and being met by the world and by all dimensions of being.

Day 7

Ego as a protective territory:

No room for enthusiasm—being filled with God, with Spirit as we experience life.

It often takes a wound to puncture the shell of the ego. The wound is an ego wound. The soul cannot be wounded or damaged. The wound can open us to the hidden treasures of the soul—to the richness of the spiritual life. Wounds can expose us to the world and to the sacred, revealing the fragility of the ego structure—if we will only allow ourselves to meet the Divine.

I reflected on the way fears and the impulse to hide pull us into a contracted realm of suffering.

Day 7

Our fears of the unknown, of death, are an energetic presence which haunts our life and can exile us from our natural love, belonging, and peace. This presence traps us in the world of the material, the mental, and the emotional. Escaping into the spiritual only works if we open to the unknown, meet the world fully and make death our ally. Otherwise our efforts are a flight into fancy, always being haunted by fear, not true spiritual transformation. By attending to our fears and our flaws, we can penetrate them to the vitality trapped there and release a great creative and vital force that promotes our growth (feeds our growth) and serves the sacred and our community.

The task is to explore what is hidden beneath (behind) these fears and to bring forth the radiance and fire that are waiting to be set free.

As we look deeply into death, we become familiar with all of its faces for us. As we move beyond our fear of death, then our physical death does not come as a thief stealing our life but as a friend in service of a greater aspect of being.

As I look deeply into fear—fears of pain, loss, discomfort, and death—I realize how fear entrances me into a false reality. It can make mere fancies a powerful force affecting my entire sense of self, the world, and well-being.

Fear often compels us to assert control, being protective of things that are not of deeper value. When we open and let go of these things, we become free to love and celebrate what is of true value. Our deep love is revealed as we meet and are met by the Divine presence—our true nature.

I find that when I am truly myself, authentic and open (not reactive), then I feel in rhythm with the music of my soul. I dance on the firm ground of my being rather than struggling to maintain a persona. I am still learning how to be myself.

I think about an old story from India of a man petrified with fear by the shape of a snake in the shadows of night; only in the light of day does he realize it is an old rope. We all get immobilized by fear of many harmless things in our mind or from the past which we have inflated into monsters to terrorize or haunt our daily life.

John O'Donohue calls fear a kind of fog which spreads and hides the true shape of things.

Through my own introspection and my work with people, I have found a few core fears.

Fear of death.

Fear of endless pain.

Fear of going mad—completely fragmenting.

Fear of not existing.

Fear of not mattering at all—being totally insignificant.

Fear of being alone/lonely forever.

Day 6

Hiding: hiding behind image/persona; hiding so I won't be ignored or rejected.

Image creates a boundary for superficial contact, controlled contact.

Hiding my doubt, my fears, my feelings of alienation and disconnection (when they are there, which is rare) sometimes my anger, my disappointments, my hopes, my ugliness, my greed, my desires, my reactive mechanical self (hidden by a mechanical, seemingly real image).

Day 7

The deeper nature or Essence which is unseen (hidden) is a gift. It must be fearlessly or at least courageously unwrapped and opened.

What we realize is that what was hidden was not hiding but in plain view, but rather we were blinded by our hiding. Trying to remain unseen, we could not see.

My first steps into the wisdom dimensions are when I place myself in the middle of whatever or whoever intimidates me. I keep going back until I have befriended the situation or grown to include it in my world. In those moments I feel alive in the meeting and feel gratitude for having such wonderful and formidable things and people on my plate.

Standing naked and authentic and grounded in the meeting is transforming. Self-revelation, however, can often be a vanity, a self-preoccupation, and a way of getting attention while really hiding.

Our habitual reality is mostly preoccupied with the sensory dimensions of being. One of the paths to the sacred involves seeing the impermanence and limitations of the sensory. Many powerful approaches examine the nature of physical reality, time, and space. In particular I recommend the brilliant work of Tarthung Tulku.[22] We can also explore the nature of habitual reality from the perspective of our emotional and psychological impulses. One reason this is important is that we live in a culture in which we are so caught up in our own inner processes that we have difficulty being present, even with the material world.

Fear As a False Deity

If we look deeply at our everyday habits, we will see fear and longing lurking in much of what we do, haunting how we move, what we say, our posture, our tone of voice, our actions, our drives, our accomplishments, our failures, our boredom, our relief, and our joys.

When we let our deepest fears guide our actions, our relationships, and our way of being, we are hostage to those fears. Our soul cries out for aliveness and lived experience rather than safety and emotional survival. At heart, we do not want our gravestone to read, "Here lies So-and-So, who succeeded for his or her whole life in avoiding what he or she feared would happen, and shrank from finding out what he or she most feared to know."

We may even go so far as to fear fear, avoiding even the examination of that highly charged area. Yet an important reason for working with fears is that our uncomfortable emotions are often where the juice of our aliveness is happening. Every distressing emotion is a call to attend to something that matters. Each is a reflected and distorted image of some core concern that holds the keys to a more authentic way of being and relating.

There are many types of fear of the unknown. These include the fear of what we are unwilling to know about ourselves—what we have disowned, what we cannot accept about ourselves, and what we do not know how to know and to use.

Cutting through Beliefs and Reactive Self-Images

The skill of inquiry is the precise application of our mind to the layers of mental/emotional crust that hide our core of wisdom and buffer us from the direct experience of the present moment. In my own life, I have uncovered countless ways I tried to protect myself from imaginary threats in an effort to secure a sense of well-being.

A major agenda in my life has been the need to be highly competent and very "good" in order to feel worthwhile and to have a place in the world. In this struggle, I would use my mental gifts to perform well in the eyes of others.

For example, when I was in my second year at the University of California, I enrolled in a fourth-year class on constitutional law, taught by a brilliant and an extremely tough professor. For the first two or three weeks of the semester, I sat quietly observing and analyzing his lines of reasoning, and garnering examples of what to do and not to do from watching others. Only after I was sure of myself did I finally enter into legal arguments with him. I succeeded in winning my point and gaining his respect. It was only then that I felt that I belonged in the class and had something to offer.

Years later, as I struggled to excel at being director of a research institute and professor myself, I realized that I was hostage to insecurities and my need to prove myself. At that time my first spiritual teacher, Chögyam Trungpa Rinpoche, pointed out that I needed to give all that up, including my need to prove myself in spiritual work.

There is always something that holds us back, some image that we are attached to or feel needs to be realized before we can give ourselves over to life and be safe. This is what must be confronted, penetrated, and transformed. In spiritual practice, all the accomplishments, successes, failures, and frustrations are evaporated by the laser of our unrelenting inquiry and our burning desire to live a life of meaning and leave a beneficial legacy.

Meals As Practice
As teeth crush a grape,
The palette sings a sweet melody.
Every cell, even hairs,
Sigh in praise.

—Martin Lowenthal, Dark Retreat 2001

In a retreat, when we eat, we take the time to be mindful in ways that amplify the activity and sanctify it.

Day 5
Eating to feed not only the body but the capacity of the soul.

Feeding not the ego but the dedication wisdom and compassion body.

Each bite feeds the larger community when we are dedicated. Feeding a larger story, not the personal ego story (vanity story).

Extracting the sacred spirit from food through conscious presence and purpose.

As I ate, each taste was sensed as energy in my heart and in my body and being. The soup, the salad, my sweet potato, all became food for the gods. Every mouthful was an offering and tasted remarkably delicious. Like a nectar.

With this practice we become not only mindful, but aware that what we eat needs to serve our larger purpose in life.

Blessings help consecrate food for this purpose.

Day 8

As I had my protein drink, I sensed feeding the body of the community, the body of the sacred, the body of nature, the body of wisdom, the body of ancestors, the body of teachings, body of teachers, the body of life, the body of the divine.

All of these bodies are entered through the heart. The heart is a gateway.

Day 6

Woke with a sore neck and jaw and eyes hurt.

Did morning blessing and body wake up (rubbing all over and tapping key points). Long, pounding shower.

Kept relaxing and maintaining a sense of presence in my heart.

Am making every action sacred and dedicated to larger community and the Divine, to Wisdom Spirit of the world. I wash, urinate, drink, exercise, and meditate with this sense.

Now I find as my attention gets distracted, I remember my presence faster. Often within seconds. My body is feeling alive and vibrant at even a cellular level. My relaxed and less rigid approach this morning meant that my before-breakfast practice lasted all morning—more than four hours. I shifted my sitting position periodically, changing which leg was on top of my half-lotus, but by the end of so many hours, I had to pry my legs apart.

On the mornings when I would wake up with a neck ache or headache or some kind of stiffness, which seems to happen for me periodically during these retreats, I would try to use the pain as a reminder to be conscious. I would use exercise and massage to release the tension in muscles. In early retreats I resisted taking aspirin out of some misplaced sense of purity. Now, when it seems appropriate, I would make it a sacred support of my work. I have found that as I age, even though I try to stay in good physical shape, my bones, joints, and muscles are not as flexible, resilient, and forgiving.

Age is also a factor for me in doing some of the Tibetan yogas, particularly the ones that involve flying into the air from a full lotus and landing in a seated lotus. Not having learned these practices in childhood and adolescence like many of the Tibetan monks, I do not have the physical and mental infrastructure to accomplish these gymnastic feats.

Day 6

Small rainbows and Clear Light in front of me are common now. More frequent are the times that they fill all space.

Visions, clear as day, have periodically been appearing for the last couple of days while I am meditating and simply resting. Often they are of landscapes, quilt patterns, and mandalas. Once I thought the covering over the window had been removed. I could see the yard of the neighbor and the woods at the back of our house. I blinked and the vision remained. These visions are not like imaginary scenes that I can create in my head. They appear outside of me in the same way the rainbow lights appear.

Sometimes when dark retreatants first have experiences of lights that show up externally without any external source, they think there are light leaks in the room. When we began doing retreats at our center in converted rooms, we kept some black electrical tape for covering leaks in the curtains we set up. At the end of one retreat, we found at least twenty pieces of tape stuck on the walls where the retreatant had thought there was light coming in from the outside.

With experienced practitioners, the visions are vividly life-size and are recognized as arising from the natural state. They are witnessed and dissolve back into the natural state. Over time they include teachers, deities, and beings from the sacred dimensions of awareness. They may also involve visions of the future.

Day 7

Long practice this morning. Then took a longer nap than usual.

Green and red lights prominent during the yoga practices related to the bardos and the realms.

Sense that third eye, inspiration point, heart center, and base are increasingly open.

I can feel the support of the energy stream of the teachings, teachers, community, and wisdom beings (qualities).

The first week has been going by very quickly. Can I train myself to embody what I am experiencing now and be able to bring it outside the retreat and into my life and teachings? It is difficult remaining fully present in here. How can I do it when I am bombarded with so many outside stimuli, responsibilities, and temptations? Part of my practice in here is to write, remaining in the natural state, talk with Karen in that way, and recall teachings in full presence.

2nd Meditation Session

Intro-structure then freestyle—did what flowed and seemed right or worth exploring. This included:

He Hing (chant)

Gazing postures

Celebration in addition to refuge. Different heart posture. Celebrating teachings, teachers, community, nature, wisdom qualities.

Realized how important and challenging it is to stay fresh when doing practices four times a day, day after day.

There is always an edge to where we are. Life is a constant flickering flame, poised on the edge, burning between two unknowns—the unknown before birth and the unknown of death and beyond. Staying poised on that edge keeps us fresh and alert. That edge is always moving like the horizon as we sail on the ocean of life experience.

Our habit is to be constantly preparing for life rather than living it. Instead of meeting life and living it fully, we reactively put conditions in

---

the way, obscuring and dulling the edge and limiting our soul. Living on the edge opens us and the entire process of life.

When our ground of being is the open nature of our soul, life is a continual journey to new horizons, to new edges—moment to moment. Hidden behind the face of the monstrous challenges of our fears, afflictions, and struggles is the radiant, welcoming soul presence inviting us to come home.

Retreat As Part of a Community

A student who brought me a meal reported that both he and his wife have been more consistent and stronger in their practices since I began my retreat.

Another student said she has felt my presence in her practice and that it has improved greatly since I have been in retreat. There is a growing sense of how my practice and retreat and the practice of everyone in the community are a service to each member and the community as a whole.

As the community meditated upstairs, I meditated along with them down in the retreat room. Strong sense of mutual support. What a wonderful blessing. I held each person in my heart during my meditation.

We are connecting and working mutually at a dimension of being that is collective, non-separate, and which weaves a rich tapestry from the efforts we all make.

During the retreat, I would speak with students briefly when they brought me meals. Over the years, people have consistently reported that my retreats have encouraged them to be more conscious, improved the commitment and quality of their practices, and have stimulated them to share about the retreats with others who have no experience of such practices but who then become interested. At my first teaching after the 1997 retreat, the meditation hall was filled and overflowed into the hallway with people who came to celebrate my return and to share in the energy of the experience.

Over the years, I have come to understand that my retreats and the retreats of others contribute to the environment of people supporting the retreat and those in the community. A dark retreat builds both individual and community capacity. In the dark retreat I came to know that I was giving other people pause with my own pause. I was offering possibilities to others as I explored them myself. I was inspiring them even as I was being inspired by them. I was evoking their dedication even as I worked with mine. I carried some of their hopes and dreams and authentic spiritual longings even as they carried mine in their hearts and minds. We mutually carried concerns and fears even as we worked to bring our deepest aspirations to fruition. We were intimately connected through our separation and our fates were somehow intertwined even as I worked individually.

Retreats and other dedicated endeavors reveal the power of individual actions to nourish and shape a community. The power of the individual is not to be different but to make a difference, not to be expressive but to be significant, not to be unconstrained but to be responsible, not to be critical but to be grateful, not to reject but to be encouraging, not to have but to be and do, not to be acknowledged but to recognize, not to accumulate but to grow, not to stave off death but to make death an ally, not to imagine but to envision, not to grasp but to contain, not to control life but to host and be hosted by life.

In the retreat I always felt connected to the community, to loved ones, and to the world. Of course the connection to the beyond, to the Divine, is most prominent and is what I worked with most. What was a bit surprising was the intimate sense of connection to other people, to nature, to my ancestry, and to a lineage of practitioners going back thousands of years.

In this context, it is clear how solitude is totally different from loneliness. John O'Donohue points out that "sometimes when you're lonely, you are very taken up with the idea of your own separation. Whereas solitude, rather than being a withdrawal, is actually an entry into and a coming home to your own deepest belonging."[23]

Day 8

Looking deeply can mean moving attention to soul dimensions of awareness and being.

Looking and finding dimensions of community, of interbeing, of the sacred.

In dark retreat I am finding that many of these dimensions have their own kinds of luminosity or radiance.

Had erotic dream last night which I used in a tantric way. Worked with sexual energies. Powerful arousal. Part of the time I worked with Taoist sexual practices that I learned from Master Chia. Most of the time I used the amplified energy to feed a sense of heart presence. Brilliant lights, at times rainbows. Maintained a clear calm center most of the time. The calm openness was there even as I experienced high energy and tingling aliveness.

Had some concern about having a wet dream. Have been able to retain my seminal fluids for several weeks now, including in lovemaking with Karen before the retreat. The work with these energies and impulses is very sacred and spiritually enhancing when approached with the right heart posture and practices. Otherwise these energies can be distracting and seductive and can become addictive.

Working with dreams and with sexual energies has been a practice of mine for nearly twenty years. In the dreamwork, being conscious and doing practice in the dream has been a powerful support to my overall growth. In this case I was able to combine both dreaming and Taoist sexual practices.

In Taoist sexual practices, like certain Tibetan tantric practices, the generative energy of the sexual organs and fluids (called *"ching"* or "essence") has the potential to vitalize and transform our bodymind and is considered the energetic source of creativity. For Taoists, sexual energy is a refined and very powerful distillation of the universal elements—earth, air, fire, and water—that not only gives us the power to physically re-create ourselves, but, when mixed with the energy of our organs and further refined by spiritual practice, also provides the juice for cultivating our spirit.

In the Taoist and tantric systems, any experience, desire, emotion, or force can be used for spiritual growth. The principle is to consciously and intentionally work with these energies with the clarity of the natural state and channel them within the body in ways that transform us from a body of reactive habits to an expression of wisdom and divine radiance. The sexual energies are considered to be the most powerful and transformative of the internal capacities that we possess. The careful arousal of desire, the systematic use of the activated energies, the retention of seminal fluid, the conservation of ovarian energy, the extension of orgasm, and the exchange of male and female energies all employ sexual energy in the conscious acceleration of spiritual growth for each partner.

> Some reflections from the day:
> Spontaneity—a freshness that is the enemy of the ego-identity. True spontaneity is our nature manifesting in the unique situation of the moment.
> Because we think we know something, it remains unknown. What we think we know about a thing or a person keeps us from discovering what and who is really here.
> The truly spiritual is not far away, as if we must journey to it. It is here. It is entwined and interwoven with everything. It is a matter of shifting our gaze, highlighting what is hidden by ordinary light.
> When we cultivate a wisdom quality we are really creating a well to tap, an endless source of fluency and nourishment.

Day 9

All wisdom qualities are elements of all other wisdom qualities. For example, hosting, interbeing, and relating are aspects of love. Freedom, unperturbability, and openness are also aspects of love. So are radiance, generosity, fearlessness, freshness, peace, harmony, wonder, and authenticity. Wisdoms are facets of the crystal of each particular wisdom, which are all facets of Essence, or Divine Wisdom.

As distracting thoughts arise, I use the tantric method of bringing sacred awareness and energy to them. Rather than viewing them as a pollution of the sacred, I treat each occurrence as the opportunity to make it sacred, to see the sacred side of the distraction—for everything is sacred if viewed correctly. There is nothing that is not Divine. This is a transforming process that cultivates the sacred.

At other times in my practice, I simply allow each thought to spontaneously dissolve into Essence, into Clear Light.

Day 10

Today is cleanup day. Changed the bedding and put out a bag of laundry which Karen said she would do.

Meditation is steady. Some mandalas appeared.

Thoughts seem to come and go, punctuating great long abiding. They do not grab my attention as much and simply dissolve into the clear abiding. Like bubbles floating to the surface of a pond, bursting when they reach the surface, and dissolving in space.

Feel immersed in the landscapes of the dark. The landscape of the room, of my thoughts and feelings when those arise, and the landscape of a deeper heart space are vast. It is also a landscape which, because there is no visual differentiation, is defined by the experience in time.

Time in the dark is also not differentiated in detail. There are long stretches to a single moment. Time is more rhythms of the body, of practice, of the dance of the soul, all held within the sense of the eternal.

What if our emotional apparatus is really meant to give us the capacity to connect, receive, and experience the vibrations of the gods—beings in the soul dimension? If we are or become open beyond our self-preoccupation—lose ourselves—we participate in the vibration of those beings. When we listen to music our hearts can dance. The joy we feel is not personal so much as the joy of the gods finding a vehicle in us, and we are gifted.

Silence is so important. Not so much the absence of outer noise, but the quiet of our own minds. As we have made life so personal, we have increased the population in our heads and amplified the sound. This prevents us from hearing the songs and rhythms of the universe. We miss the music of the spheres—not the outer, but the inner, non-personal, heavenly spheres, the music of the soul.

Perhaps there are feelings that are simply reactions and basic personal responses, and then there are those that are gifts from the gods. This is the difference between fun and true delight. Fun is involving and personal, and delight is more transcendent and connective and includes the gift of wonder and awe. Fun may become delight, but delight can arise in many ways.

We open to the gifts of the gods when we pray, dance, sing, have true humor, make music, and enjoy the gift of life itself. Then we experience God's joy.

The vibrant stillness, radiant darkness, and thundering silence were all reminders that everything is alive. The world only becomes dead to us when we do not relate and understand.

Day 11

Early meditation today lacked a kind of sharpness—not really dull, but simply not as vivid as some other times. Yet afterward, everything seemed clear, quiet, and alive. Sometimes the practice is great and the non-practice time is dull or agitated. Other times, the practice is more routine and the rest of the time is fresh, alive, open, and inner silence. Sometimes both are dull or agitated and occasionally both are great.

Some circular rainbows. Most of the time they are like straight rays in front of me. Other times the rainbow is like a radiating star in front. The circles were somewhat above eye level.

Often the gold that is yielded in meditation comes in unexpected ways, at unexpected times, and in unpredictable places. If anything, our expectations are a barrier to discovering the hidden treasures of the soul. Just as the light of day blinds me to the inner lights, so the torch of expectation obscures the luminous gifts of the moment of spontaneous experience.

It is as if the beauty, shape, and nature of the spiritual hides from the glare of our concepts and ideas about what should happen. It takes a gentle, open gaze to reveal what had been in shadow in the spotlight of the mental.

In this dark retreat, as in the last one, I have felt completely at home in the heart of connection and belonging which is sometimes shielded in relationships by hopes and fears and agendas for interaction.

Doing this retreat allows me the time to not just glimpse or touch on the deeper places, but to dwell there in a way that is nourishing, strengthening, and renewing. This is true of my daily meditation and it is amplified tenfold in a retreat.

In the abiding at the end of practice this afternoon, my nostrils were filled with the fragrance of an exquisite fruitlike nectar. I was in another world.

One of the roles of a spiritual friend is to remind us that all that we need is close at hand, just beneath the surface of the appearances of our lives. That with silence, listening, opening, hosting, we can return to the hearth of the spiritual home.

When we look and listen deeply we can open with a gentleness and kindness beyond our fears and impoverished expectations about what is in the depths. To work with the full richness of the sacred, it sometimes helps to have a language of words, images, and sounds that evokes the vitality of our wisdom nature and places us in a frame of mind to see, hear, and feel the shimmering of the world.

4 In the Flow

Sunrise in Dark Retreat

As the sun of conscious memory rises
above the horizon of slumber,
It brings the objects of my world back into being—
bed, night stand, cushion.
In this room of darkest night,
there is no need of shadows.

—Martin Lowenthal, Dark Retreat 2001

Day 12

Slept well for the first time in a while. I think I have solved the pillow problem that has been giving me a sore neck and jaw.

Awoke very early, probably before three.

I have become much more aware of sensations and a sense of presence in the back of my body.

When I do various parts of practice they often evoke luminous lights from my heart center as well as in space (in a way the same). For example, when I do the concluding dedication of merit to all beings and the community, I sense white and sometimes a light that is sky-blue.

The senses are receptive from two directions—the outer world and the inner. When directed outward, they allow us to experience the world, to receive information, and to act. When directed inward, they give us the means to experience and express the inner life—of the mind, the emotions, and the spiritual. Examples of the inner are when we imagine something and feel as though it is happening. It is how we feel our emotions and get excited about something.

The senses are active and projective as well as passive and receptive.

The spiritual can only speak to us when other dimensions of our being are relatively silent and in balance, or when we are trained to attend to them all simultaneously even when they are heightened.

One difficulty is that we live in an age and culture in which the aggressive assault and seduction of the visual and of sound insists on so much attention. In addition, our self-preoccupations and concerns for our own wants, fears, and emotions seem vital, important, and even essential. Lost in all this is the truly essential, the spiritual, the sacred, the true home of our being and the real source of our destiny.

We have entire industries devoted to the seduction of the senses, to the outer power of images, sounds, and things. Other industries are dedicated to the reduction of life experiences to emotions, personal history, emotional release, and salvation. All this dislocates our attention, energies, and self-sense into a surface dimension of life, hiding the rich and sacred that can only be revealed by looking, listening, and sensing deeply.

A deep sense of impoverishment is felt as the superficiality of our social reality and the turmoil of the inner mental and emotional reality is always haunted by the longing for belonging, joy, and the filling of our spiritual void.

One of the reasons for the high level of stress in modern life is that so little attention is given to the silent, flowing, and open dimensions of our being which are comforting, nourishing, and inspiring. We access these dimensions by becoming clear—clear about the distinctions between the dimensions of our being, clear that the surface level of our ordinary reactive awareness is not reality, clear of distractions and interference of mental chatter, and clear as a way of being like a calm lake where everything that is not water has settled to the bottom.

The clarity I am referring to here has many aspects. The first involves slowing thought patterns so attention can be redirected and consciously used. The second is relaxing beyond the agitation and tension of emotions and seeing beyond the filters that emotions and moods place in front of the lens of perception. From these first two processes, a more open heart posture is revealed in relation to what is occurring.

In order to develop clarity, we need to work from our self-sense. Our self-sense is an awareness that is also pure presence (Essence, Spirit, Divine, God, Allah, Tao, natural mind) expressing itself through each of us. This self-sense is the starting place for all conscious work. It is not the identity, an idea about what we are, but the sense that there is someone who reads this passage, who eats meals, who has experiences, who learned to walk, who has a body, who has thoughts and emotions, who can notice minute sensations, who can feel the smallest bump on a smooth surface, who can see a landscape thousands of times the size of his or her eyes, who can imagine being in locations thousands of miles away and even millions of miles out in space, who has a sense of presence, and who can simply be without having to be somewhere.

This self-sense can also be viewed as a bridge between the world of the sensory and the sacred world of soul and spirit. These worlds are dimensions of being. For purposes of increased understanding, we can think of reality having multiple dimensions of being (and becoming) ranging from the sensory, which includes the material world and our thoughts and feelings, to the subtle or soul, which includes the formative principles, vitalizing forces, and wisdom qualities, and to Essence, which is the ground and substance, the potential and the manifestation of all that is, beyond and immanent in all that is.

All life has the dimensions of this "nest of being." Experientially, we as human beings have the capacity to be a conscious bridge between the dimensions and to cultivate the qualities of the sensory and the sacred.

Learning Being

One way to think about this is that each of us is a learning being who has a psycho-physical bodymind and is a part of Essence. This learning being is open, malleable, impressionable, and has the ability to pattern information, and not only to have a self-sense, but to be self-conscious.

The learning being is often called the "mind." In our materially dominated world, many equate this with the brain but in many spiritual traditions it is based in the heart center. From a spiritual point of view, all the senses, of which brain functioning is one, are a kind of functional consciousness that is part of sensory awareness, which is in turn rooted in the sacred awarenesses.

Whereas the Essence dimension of our being is unaffected by experience and events, the learning being is always affected by outside forces until it merges with Essence. The learning being has the job of operating in the world and living life. It is the aspect of who we are that creates meaning and can grow. As it formulates ideas and patterns actions into behaviors, we could say that it forms a body of habits. This habit body includes both the mental and physical habits which we develop over the course of this life (and, according to some traditions, which we have also accumulated from past lives in the form of tendencies).

The learning being is both the experiencer and the maker of meaning. By making meaning out of experience, it transforms experience according to its intentions, capacity, and training. The world is naturally rich and sacred. When we react to our experience with fear, alienation, or resentment, we make lead. When we embrace and open to experience directly and lovingly, we experience the gold of wisdom and feed the sacred dimensions, which include ourselves, our communities, and all beings.

The learning being is always transforming the material of raw experience through a personally constructed mental, emotional, and spiritual digestive system. In a sense, it is like what our physical digestive system does with food. We eat a carrot and it is broken down into vitamins, phytochemicals, sugars, starch, and various minerals. These are processed in the mouth, stomach, intestines, liver, and bloodstream so that organs in the body are nourished. The body has the mechanisms and rules for making use of the food so that it can grow. In the same way, once a set of rules and structures is in place for making meaning and framing experience, our attention is directed automatically and the meaning is extracted that feeds our habit body.

In terms of the physical body, these learning processes are essential for our survival because we have little instinctual information at birth to assist us in the material world. While the source of aliveness and the impulse to grow come from the sacred dimensions, the attention in early life is mostly to the sensory domain because that is the time for learning how to live physically, socially, and emotionally. In this way, our sensory/intellectual consciousness becomes highly developed.

The body of habits formed in early life which were based on limited cognitive capacity and the needs of a child must be outgrown and reformulated if we are to mature and move through the stages and passages of life. Even at early ages, we are at some level aware that there are other aspects of life which are based in the spiritual.

The learning being, when oriented toward the physical, mental, and emotional, forms the habit body of identity, often called the ego. This comes from the sense that reality is based in the physical and in our personality, and results in continual thoughts and feelings which reinforce our egocentric heart postures. Because this frame is characterized by polarized concepts and a sense of separation, fear, and longing, we become hostage to its limitations and frustrated by our attempts to stabilize what is inherently changeable and temporary.

When the learning being orients toward the spiritual and includes the sacred dimensions of awareness, it is freed from the prison of ego limitations.

Presence

Once we experience and fully integrate the principle of hosting presence, we have the foundation for understanding and accessing any wisdom presence. The principle of presencing is the same and applies to all forms of wisdom. It is similar to understanding the principles of multiplication. When we know that three times three is nine; the same principle is known to be true of pears, oranges, chickens, books, tapes, and shirts: Three times three of anything always yields nine.

The key to hosting presence is not intellectual understanding; it is consciousness. When we consciously include presencing in our attention, then it is real and operates through us. Once we experience it, we know it is always so. However, it does little good to realize it once and simply forget to practice it and to then talk about it as if we know about it. The only value the truth of hosting presence has is the extent to which it is realized. Bringing this to everyday life and being nourished by it depends on our capacity to maintain the sense of presence moment to moment.

However we describe or relate to Essence/Spirit—the Divine—and no matter how much we have read, heard, talked about, and theorized about it, it is conscious awareness, the actual feeling and realization of hosting presence that is necessary for us to experience that presence. The Divine is space, and fills all space and time, and includes and animates all forms with the qualities of radiance. It is the presence within which and through which all presences arise.

The fact that presence is always everywhere is of no use until we realize it through our aliveness. It is like electrical energy. It is every-where but of no use to us until it is marshaled and connected in some way that gives it direction and application.

Love

Beyond conscious attention, it is our love that brings the current of presence to life. We experience this love in glimpses at times of romantic love. If we sense deeply, we can tap this capacity for love of life in other activities. When we intentionally engage in an activity that we love, we bring objects, actions, and relationships to life. We animate the entire situation and practice the art of dedication and the power of presence.

As we tap the wellspring of energy in our natural way of being and sense of presence, we relate to our entire environment of people, objects, and places with our aliveness. Everything is fresh and sacred, vital and vibrant, as we sense the presence of creation in all things.

The entire world can teach us about aliveness. When we truly relate to objects and nature, they cease to be inanimate and become a living presence. We sense this intuitively and thus we often give names to our cars, our houses, favorite plants, and our computers.

I remember in the early years of my meditation practice I would meditate on an oak tree that rose majestically outside my window. For years that tree was my companion and teacher. It was not that it spoke to me or I read the great mysteries in its bark. More accurately, I accessed ways of knowing and insights by opening to its presence and letting that presence work me. It came to life in my deeper world as I let it touch me and awaken wisdoms and qualities that languished beneath the surface of my everyday habits of thoughts and feelings.

The power of presence includes the power to invest our landscape, our tools, and our activities with spiritual powers. We make the world a temple where people, things and settings have spiritual relevance.

In the Old Testament the lower world is called "sheol," which is the realm of diminishing being. As Jacob Needleman says: "Sheol is the condition of human life proceeding with ever-diminishing human presence. It is the movement toward *absence*, the movement away from God—for let us carefully note that one of the central definitions of God that is given in the Old Testament is *conscious presence*. Moses asks God, 'What shall I say to the people of Israel? Whom shall I say has sent me with these commandments?' The answer he receives, as mysterious today as it has ever been: 'Say unto the children of Israel, I AM has sent me unto you'" (Exodus 3:14).[24]

When we are totally preoccupied with and run by the sensory world, we lose the sense of the greater presence which is the sacred. We lose perspective and relate everything to our personal stories. We lose the source of enduring meaning, love, and satisfaction.

The task is to live in both worlds, honoring each in its own way and realizing that the source of true aliveness and joy arises from the sacred. The outer life of physical and social needs of mortal beings must be considered real, but secondary (not evil or irrelevant). We must be willing to engage our sensory/material and sacred/spiritual natures, holding both and opening ourselves to the transcendentally reconciling force of grace—the gift of God, of Essence.

Grace

Like hosting, grace is another way of talking about Essence—the Divine, God. We know grace through the experience of awe and wonder. We know grace through the unknown. We know grace through the miraculous nature of life. We know grace in the smile of an infant, in the fragrance of an Easter lily, in the calling of the loon, and in the peace in our own heart when we open unconditionally to a living moment. We know grace when we save an injured bird, nurse a newborn, shape a pot on a wheel, sing a song, or offer a helping hand to someone in need.

We cannot locate it or define it. It is both a force and the space within which the force manifests all around us and through us. Grace both emanates from all that is to us and emanates from us to all that is.

The sense of grace moves us beyond our self-centered concerns into the world of the sacred. It is deep-seated, familiar, and close, and is known through intimate witnessing. As we relax into the space of the intimate witness and into the sense of hosting awareness, we see that life expresses itself in each moment as energy, as experience, as action. Out of the alchemical process of our attention, hosting presence, and conscious engagement, the energy of creation arises out of the moment. This is union of grace and self, of love and desire, of action with divine harmony, of energy and openness; it is the alchemical marriage.

In order for that transformation to take place we must cross the sense of boundary between everyday content awareness and the hosting awareness which includes our open and radiant wisdom presence. Until we make that crossing, we tend to experience ourselves in our heads and deep inside us. The transformation involves the shifting of our center of gravity to the heart. This occurs as we release the grip of hopes, fears, frustrations, and assertion and relax into the open, awakened qualities of being. The key to entering the heart center is maintaining some of our attention in our spiritual awareness and manifesting our wisdom energy in the service of the world.

Eventually, we must seek the wisdom of grace everywhere, not simply by going inside. The idea of an inner world that is separate from an outer world is an illusion. The distinction between inner and outer may be temporarily useful because we begin our spiritual paths with the sense of separation. Along the way, we simply penetrate the shell of this artificial distinction to experience that at the core, all conceptual distinctions dissolve in the wholeness of all that is, in the undivided nature of hosting.

All of this comes from a desire to grow continuously. When Jesus said "Become as little children," he did not mean to be helpless or inca-pable of reason and thought. He was referring to the spiritual plane. We need to relate to our hunger for wisdom and the nourishment of the spirit in the persistent way a child seeks the milk of the mother. We are reaching for the nourishment of the divine mother.

Silence, like the dark, is an embracing and vast companion. Silence can host sound, and in profound silence everything can be included. One gateway to this silence is a gentle, open listening from the back of the head.

Silence is the traveling companion of clarity. In listening to the silence not only are things uncovered and revealed, but because they are hosted, they can become clearer.

Day 13

A real solid practice day. This came after a night of numerous dreams including one where I was involved in the trial of a Nazi war criminal, one who had run concentration camps. It was in 1948 and I was working on the trial outwardly, and inwardly working on being able to retain my own humanity along with his in my perspective. At another point in the dream, a young gentile girl is explaining quite well to other children what the Holocaust was about, or at least what hap-pened.

Spent part of the afternoon doing mindfulness using the breath. The quality of presence is profound. I want to reinforce to my students to do this practice at the beginning of their retreats. It is useful to do periodi-cally even when doing Dzogchen and tantra.

Sometimes when I plan a schedule of practices, the habit of antici-pation and waiting seems so strong. In this mode I am thinking of what comes next even as I begin and do one practice. The activity is a kind of waiting until what is anticipated comes along. At that point my mind can already be on to the next future event or events. Anticipation is closed and spoils freshness and openness; waiting kills the experi-ence of the moment. Sometimes this is not so obvious but haunts the present from the background. This anticipatory mind is a product of putting the mental organizer and planner in charge and giving in to its desire for control.

Day 14

During morning chi kung I enjoyed some unusual fragrances—a kind of delightful and refreshing citrus fragrance. This is the first time that has come during this practice.

This month of retreat is about half over and it is going so very quickly. Part of me feels that there is not enough time left to finish training myself to embody all the wisdom qualities that will truly be of service. It is going to take so much to really master my mind and body. How can I surrender completely if I cannot even let loose of my anticipatory thinking?

In this retreat I feel like I am at a banquet of senses, ideas, feelings, gods and goddesses, and wisdom energies. I am trying to experience and do justice to this feast of spiritual delight.

One of the dangers in some approaches to spirituality is that we try to reduce everything to a monoscape, a single neutral color, odor, sound, or feel. Much like what commercial culture does with foods, architecture, TV, etc.

Day 15

Experienced a sense of full-body, cellular presence while doing t'ai chi.

During abiding and many of the practices, there is a vast sense of presence. It is not that my senses and my presence have expanded; rather, as I open and surrender, this greater presence fills my senses and expands me or uses me to manifest.

I reflected on the paradoxes of life and my tendency to fight them or prematurely resolve them.

It is one of the paradoxes of life that those unwanted feelings, thoughts, and attitudes which we try to exorcise or perform a kind of inner surgery on will simply reassert themselves, as if strengthened by our unsuccessful efforts. I have found that the surest way of working with these uncomfortable parts of our lives is to relate to them, know them, host them, transform them, and discover the gifts they bring to life from the spiritual depths. Each of these "negative" feelings is a clue and a gateway to an aspect of presence that has been hidden, avoided, or ignored. Instead of being put off by their apparent ugliness, we need to be challenged to quest for the beauty that is being protected by these fierce guardians who rightly or wrongly have been protecting the temple of the soul.

Working with all the competing parts of our personalities and the dimensions of being is about allowing an integrity to emerge. Integrity is about wholeness and about everything being true to itself, the whole and each part having its rightful place. When we are confused about our integrity, we feel split and divided against ourselves and the world. This makes us vulnerable to all kinds of destructive and desperate impulses and reactions.

We cannot force this integrity to occur. If we do, we make it conceptual, an identity of the ego. This forced unity will crack and split apart when tested by the pressures of life, or it will drive us into righteous rages and battles to defend our fortresses of sand. Only by hosting, becoming intimate with all parts of ourselves and by letting the sacred emerge and gather all aspects into an integral, unified presence, can real integrity and harmony manifest. This process of including and holding is one of the ways we can let the soul care for us.

Day 16

Last night a friend who brought dinner also included some very rich chocolate cake. I ate about half and left the rest for Karen. What a mistake to eat the little I did. The caffeine and sugar are really foreign to me and kept me awake for hours. Additionally, the Brussels sprouts of the dinner gave me terrible gas. I was still passing wind this morning.

Whether because of these conditions or in spite of them, I don't know, but my practice this morning was alert, alive, and stable. The sweet fragrances of the other states of being that I go into during practice were prevalent throughout, even overcoming the gas of the sprouts.

Day 17

Awoke early and started out good. Then Karen came down during an early meditation and, speaking through the closed door, needed some extensive help using my online mail to contact her nephew in Chile, where she is headed in four days.

The interruption was significant and it took a lot of willpower to start up again for a complete session. It took a while to settle in and I was glad I did. At the end I felt more present and energized.

The process was about relaxing into the flow of the sacred versus the flow of thoughts and feelings. To do this we have to apply the will to our attention to interrupt the stream of thinking and feeling to move our attention into the spiritual dimensions of being. Once we are stabilized there, we can surrender to the currents and directions of grace and allow ourselves to be taken into the unknown.

All spiritual work requires a fine balance between will and willingness. With will we mobilize our attention and energies with determination in a direction. Will helps us to start and to sustain effort. Willingness allows us to accept and be shaped by grace. It suggests an open perspective and a heart posture of surrender in which we intentionally offer ourselves, realizing that our natural state is not at odds with life, but an authentic expression of Spirit.

Reflected on some keys to fully inhabiting our lives—to authentic presence:

Dynamic stillness
Thundering or Resounding silence
Alert Relaxation
Intimate Witnessing
Hosting the Host
Sensing from beyond inner and outer
I try to recall part of a poem of Rumi:

Tomorrow you'll see what you've broken tonight, thrashing about in the dark.

Inside you there is an artist you don't know about,

and she's not interested in how things look different in moonlight.

If you're with her unfaithfully

you're causing terrible damage. If you've opened your love to the Great Love,

You are helping people you have never known and will never see.

Is what I say true? Say yes quickly.

If you know it, you've known it since the moment before you were born.

Day 18

Up very early, needing very little sleep.

Strong practice.

Morning reflections: There are many right ways of doing things and many wrong. (Not only one way to be right or wrong in practice, as in most of life.)

Unlike the physical world where two object or things cannot occupy the same space at the same time, the spirit always inhabits the same space as the physical.

At various points during the day, I would have the thought that I have only ten more days, not as relief but a sense of urgency, a sense I need more time, more time for what is unclear. Perhaps for some lurking hope to complete spiritual realization. Perhaps a greater sense of mastery. Or maybe because it is such a simple and blessed life in here. Sure, there is a part of me that is waiting to emerge into daylight and walk in the woods and take in the sky, and gaze at the stars and moon, and feel the rocky ground under my feet and stand against a cold wind as it refreshes my skin. I also want to get on with my work—my writing, my teaching, my connections with students, and my meetings with clients. But this is such a precious interlude in the year, a true recreation and retreat and a time of devoted service.

I am reminded of Rilke's poem—"You Darkness." I think it goes:

You darkness, from which I come
I love you more than all the fires
that fence in the world
Because a fire throws a circle of light
and then no one sees beyond or
can know of you.

But the darkness pulls in everything,
figures and fires, animals and myself.
How easily it holds them—
powers and people—
And it is possible a great force is stirring near me.
I believe in nights.

Worked with inquiry—the type that leads to poise—being with an unanswerable question such as "Who are you?" This is an inquiry of the self to the self.

This is not a mental exercise but an opening to the spiritual dimensions of being and awareness. The response is not in what we say so much as in our spontaneous presence in the moment.

Inquiry

Inquiry is both a search and a way of being. It is the quest for clarity and the open experience that gives us a glimpse of home. This is particularly true of inquiries that do not have real answers.

We let inquiry take us into the mystery and then simply relate directly to the open, wondrous way of being totally present in the question. Here we use the question to open our attention and simply abide in the openness, experiencing being grounded and at home in the open, unknowing, and spaciousness of poise.

In that moment, the head and heart are united. The head uses attention and the structure of thought to create a pause and the heart provides the openness and capacity to abide and to create intimacy. We pose the question and then realize that we are the answer. Our way of being is the answer. The awareness itself is what is recovered, an awareness that has always been there. We then allow this awareness to be present in our attention and cultivate our capacity to illuminate our life with its radiance.

The process of witnessing the mind in simple inquiry meditation has been compared to observing a flock of birds. The flock, as a unit, sometimes flies straight, sometimes this way and that, sometimes in one shape and sometimes in another. As we watch the flock, our contemplative process can be expanded by including the person watching the flock in flight. Meditating often involves the shifting of our attention back and forth. Sometimes we glimpse beyond the thoughts to the process of thinking and to the space in which the thoughts arise and sometimes we don't. Sometimes we are witness and other times we are simply merged with the flock. Gradually we realize that we are both, and experience what has been called the "power of simultaneous awareness."

In directing us toward the nature of this simultaneous awareness, a question is a closer approximation of the experience than a declarative statement. A question is better able to capture the sense of including all the elements of paradox and complexity in a simple form. A question is by its nature an opening process.

Transforming the bodymind in the service of wisdom is like taming a wild horse. The horse has tremendous raw energy that we want to use. We want to marshal the passions of the horse without hurting it and without getting thrown or kicked by it. We can only approach the horse with purpose, care, attention, and a lot of persistence. We need to make friends with the horse, take charge, and be willing to take a number of wild rides in the process. The horse may fight the training and try to go back to old habits, but gradually it begins to enjoy the relationship, being ridden, and the concentration of energy that brings it to realize its real potential.

As in training a horse, the training of our minds through inquiry requires skill as we strip away the illusions of our habitual worldview and our assumptions about reality. We must not fall into the trap of mental games and nihilistic views where we believe that nothing exists. To realize that all ideas about reality are not adequate or necessarily true and that things do not inherently exist but are impermanent is not the same as saying they do not exist. We must not lose our common sense about the conventional reality of the material world which includes us and other people. We must not ignore the need for skillful and determined work in our practice or we risk greater confusion, distress, and self-preoccupation.

> In the dark, as I concentrated with the question "Who am I?" and allowed alert poise to fill my attention, every noise, scent, and touch had a deliciousness. I sensed the energy of presence in the darkness and rejoiced at the wonder of life.

When we ask the question, "Who am I?" our mind incessantly tries to come up with answers, reflective of its apparent limitless capacity for chatter. Only with stamina and determination will we finally go beyond the momentary glimpses of open hosting. The process of shifting our way of being as a result of continuous effort is often compared to that of water wearing down a hard rock.

Authentic wisdom presence is paradoxically both the result of the gradual process of spiritual growth and the spontaneous, wondrous experience of home from which we host our practice. The ways of wisdom are practiced to grow our capacity to abide in the sense of home, and our sense of home is the ground from which the ways of wisdom unfold and come to fruition.

> Did six meditation sessions today, a couple of rest periods, and two writing periods.
> It is clear that when the various elements of our body and mind are balanced, the internally generated lights of our wisdom nature can radiate through our senses. Our open attention becomes a vehicle for these illuminations and visions.

5 The Burden of Wisdom and the Wisdom of Responsibility

Bell of Compassion

Wood strikes metal.
We resonate in the world of its ringing scream,
Opened by the tear in silence.

—Martin Lowenthal,
Dark Retreat 2001

Day 19

A teaching story came in my dreams last night:

A wealthy and powerful lord surrounded himself with comforts, pleasures, and entertainment, partly because he thought that this was how a good life should be lived, and partly because it buffered and hid the fears and longings which lurked in his depth. Most of the time he could forget that he even had disturbing fears and feelings, but there was one which he knew he could not avoid, one that was more powerful than he and that had no regard for his position, one against which he could think of no defense. His fear that he could not hide from was death.

The prince decided to get help from those who would know about such subjects. He invited the three greatest spiritual masters of his realm to dine with him.

The three arrived on the appointed evening and found a great feast. Although they usually ate quite simply, they ate with delight and relish as good guests. The conversation was lively as they mostly talked with each other, and they spread a warmth and joy that swept through the prince like a wave filling an empty cove.

As they got to the dessert, the wise spiritual masters inquired about the reason for this unusual invitation. The prince told them of his fear of death and his desire to know how to face death. As they continued to eat and drink, he explained that he had read many theoretical treatises on death and was not interested in ideas. So he had devised a plan to have them teach him what they truly knew about facing death. They asked what that might be. He pointed out that it was already underway. He had a deadly poison placed in their food. This way he could learn from each of their examples.

He went on that he wanted to see if they knew ways of defeating death or whether they would be overcome with fear in spite of their teachings and practices.

The three wise masters looked at him with amazement on their faces, then looked at each other, shrugged their shoulders as if to say "oh, well!" and continued eating and enjoying the dinner conversation.

After about ten minutes, one of the masters said "excuse me," sat up, his eyes rolled up toward the heavens, a peaceful, compassionate look came to his face, he mumbled a few gratitudes and blessings, and with an ever-so-slight bow of his head, passed on. His body continued to sit but no sound came from those still lips and no heart beat in his quiet chest.

The other masters said some blessings and bowed and then continued their conversation and drank the fine liqueurs that had been brought.

The prince asked what the master had just done and the others ignored him.

After a few more minutes, a second master said "excuse me." This master also sat up with her eyes rolled to the heavens, said her gratitudes and blessings, smiled a compassionate smile, relaxed, and with a small bow of her head, left her body. The third master said a few prayers and blessings and turned to the prince.

The prince realized that the delight he had felt earlier was gone and that he was already missing the vital company of his companions. As the prince sat stupefied, trying to comprehend what he was witnessing, the deep pain of his loneliness, fears, and especially his longing came to the surface.

The third master then spoke to him in a gentle yet firm tone. "I guess I have been chosen to speak briefly about this before I pass through the great threshold to join the others. We are leaving you with three gifts.

"The first is demonstrating how to celebrate life and greet death the unknown as an old friend and ally. The second gift will get you started and motivate you to learn and master the celebration of life and the intimacy with death. This gift is the irrepressible longing which you now feel. The third gift is the blessing of responsibility for creating benefit for beings from what has occurred this evening.

"You have also taken upon yourself the work of each of us so that it may continue. This is the work of dedicating your every effort to the happiness, growth, and freedom of all beings.

"In learning to do and make real this third gift, you have a path to true joy, peace, and a way to come to your real home.

"Bless you and know that we three are now forever in your heart. If you try to forget or betray these gifts, you will be haunted by the guilt and remorse of our images. If you remain true, our presence will support and guide you every step of the way."

With that, the third master became still and silent, and left this world as had the others. Then their bodies dissolved into rainbow light.

As I write down the dream, I think of a concluding line to the story: What will you do with the gifts entrusted to you?

Another story is also unfolding around this tale. It is about my relating to it. In the dream I sensed myself as the third master and experienced the surprise of having been poisoned, the calm acceptance of that fact, and the sense of responsibility to use that fact as a tool for my own growth and passing, and to teach the prince. As I write the story, I have come face to face with the fact that I am also the prince.

As a younger student I had poisoned or killed my teachers in some subtle ways that made them even more a part of me. I experienced the boundless delight and endless love for them and their presence, and longed for the keys to their mastery. I did not know how to relate to them properly and used them in selfish ways to gain their secrets. This may be one way to receive the gift and take the responsibility as my own, having to live according to its strictures for the benefit of others. This is the path to being able to be of dedicated service to others and to the community. I know I need to honor those gifts and the givers every day of my life and am always asking for help and support to live up to what I have been given. This is true of the gifts from not only my teachers, but my parents, my first wife, my former lovers, my wife, my children, my friends, my ancestors, and my students.

Whether these gifts are blessings or burdens depends on my mood. At times it seems like an impossible task and unmovable weight. At others, I sing and dance with the opportunity and rejoice at the challenges.

The poisoning happened in various ways, from being intimidated by them, to finding fault, to competing, to getting disappointed, to resenting the attention they gave to others, through resisting what I was given, through neglecting their presence, through ambition, through anger when they didn't conform to my expectations of them, through withdrawal when I didn't understand, through fantasies of their validation of me, through simply not being fully myself with them.

As a teacher I have also experienced students doing all these things with me. I am constantly amazed at all the ways they have of refusing to meet me and of refusing the gifts being offered through me as a vehicle.

I offer this story to you as a way of sharing the gift that was passed on to me from grace in my dreamstate. This was a very powerful experience and is a very sacred story to me.

I sit in the dark in stony silence
Penetrating the black with wide eyes.

Lights flash from nowhere,
Blues and reds and green
Pulse at my naked vision.

The skin of my hands, arms, and face
Touch and are touched by the vibrating air.
My heart senses a world,
Vast beyond imagination.
My nostrils delight with each
Inhalation of the bouquet of ancient wine
Of this deep place.
I cannot tell where I begin or end
Or whether this is my experience
Or the sigh of an unknown presence.

Today unfolded differently from others. I have done less formal practice and more reflection and writing. There is a clarity and honesty to the inquiries and reflections that has been set up by the practices. The insights and revelations have deepened my inner work and enhanced the power of my formal practices. I sense being more open and an expanded embracing of my flaws.

I realize that one of the qualifications for teaching is the experience of being wounded and wounding in the deepest spiritual sense (not in trivial ways). This means a willingness to take on the burden of our teachers and to have others take it from us, making it their own. Another qualification is the ability to hold simultaneously the sorrow of our failings and the joy of being a vehicle for the wisdom energies—a channel for the Divine.

When we say it is the goal to rest in and embrace our true nature, it is important to include our nature in all dimensions of being. This includes our species nature, which is to create legacies in the world through children, work, art, exemplars, and many other ways. It is a denial of this nature to work only on and for oneself.

Day 20

A solid practice day. I was a bit scattered and my mind dreamy at the beginning but the more I practiced, the more awake, alert, and stable I became. Now, in early afternoon, after about ten hours since rising, my experience is characterized by presence, starbursts of rainbow light, white lights and deep blue lights, and there is often a sweet fragrance with a bit of a kick to it that fills the space.

I periodically find myself reciting the Yeats poem "The Song of Wandering Aengus," which is one of my favorites. The power, space, sensuousness, and love in the spiritual quest for the eternal beloved is wondrous.

The Song of Wandering Aengus

I went out to the hazel wood,
Because a fire was in my head,
And cut and peeled a hazel wand,
And hooked a berry to a thread;
And when white moths were on the wing,
And moth-like stars were flickering out,
I dropped the berry in a stream
And caught a little silver trout.

When I had laid it on the floor
I went to blow the fire aflame,
But something rustled on the floor,
And some one called me by my name:
It had become a glimmering girl
With apple blossom in her hair
Who called me by my name and ran
And faded through the brightening air.

Though I am old with wandering
Through hollow lands and hilly lands,
I will find out where she has gone,
And kiss her lips and take her hands;
And walk among long dappled grass,
And pluck till time and times are done
The silver apples of the moon,
The golden apples of the sun.[25]

From a certain viewpoint, the soul and spirit are not the gifts that are entrusted to us. The gift is life itself. It is the body, the mind, the emotions, the generative and creative impulses. It is the ability to create meaning and grant significance. It is the possibility of taking responsibility and growing. It is the vitality of relationships and community. It is the promise of home in oneself, in relationship, in nature, in the soul, and in the eternal Spirit or Essence/Divine. It is the opportunity to serve the sacred and make it manifest in new and wondrous ways.

We cannot kill the soul or the spirit but we can go between the events of birth and death not having lived. The rich garden that is given to us can wither from neglect, fear, numbing out in comfort and addiction, or being distracted and seduced by titillation.

In our secular society and in many rule- and fear-based religions, we do not learn how to be in, to celebrate, and to cultivate the sacred. The sacred needs to be part of the educational experience of children so they form the spiritual habits, sensibilities, and sense of wonder from which to live and grow and create as adults.

As part of my work in retreat, I am attuned to the suffering, conflicts, and injustices in the world, and am making concerted efforts to hold people in my heart and radiate harmonizing and compassionate energy to them and their situations. This specifically includes particular family members, friends, clients, and students. It also involves larger-scale issues of violence in all forms, injustices—racial and gender and based on sexual preferences, hatred, neglect, and exploitation. Even the grief I feel about these things is a form of celebration and has real poignancy in it. My tonglen practices have been increasingly intense.

Among the most important senses in sacred work is the imagination. It is the sense we use for inner work and to give form and meaning to what we find. It is critical to train and discipline this sense, or a number of dangers can arise. These include trivializing the world and the inner experience through fancy and fantasy. Another is letting the imagination become enlisted by our fears and angers and desires—a servant to our unbridled emotions. Another is letting it become so closed that it constructs elaborate cocoons for the energies it should be releasing and helping to grow.

In using the imagination to apprehend the sacred and to create from it, we must be clear about the dimensions of being and awareness.

Knowing how they operate, what belongs to each, and how they inter-relate when they do. One of the most common failures is the material-ization of the sacred and the assumption that the sacred can be validated by the emotional dimension, our intense emotions.

6 Making Love with the Goddess

I am asleep yet my heart is awake . . .
the voice of my beloved beats . . .
open to me
my sister
my companion
my dove
my perfect one
for my head is filled with dew
and my locks with the droplets of night

—Song of Songs 5:2

Day 21

    Last night I remained conscious and energized and did a sexual form of tantra practices with Karen as my consort—clear open awareness and presence, pure energy, and total intimacy in service of the sacred.

    Karen came to drop off some bananas. After talking through the door between the retreat bedroom/meditation room and the bathroom (which is also dark), we agree to a good-night hug. We both intuitively knew that this was a code phrase for physical intimacy.

This retreat, unlike my early retreats in the dark, includes practices designed to rest in the nature of mind, work with energies and lights, and play with an edge.

I feel excited and unreserved about the "hug." The embrace is wonderful. In the dark we see each other with touches and kisses and the clear images of the mind's eye. We engage in a dance of hands, lips, and bodies. After a short time, our few clothes are peeled away, revealing our magnetized and electrified flesh, folding into each other and gliding along the surfaces.

I am completely into this dance as I continue my practice of presence, bringing the energy of the sensations into my heart center as well as radiating them to Karen as part of this sensual "contact improv."

I have long been a practitioner of sensual and sexual tantra or yoga, using sexual energy in the cultivation of wisdom presence and transformation into a dedication body. While Karen is not involved in regular practices the way I am (both meditative and tantric) she is familiar with them and knows many of them. She knows how to engage in this dance of intimacy and support my spiritual practice.

Our explorations of each other are both familiar and freshly new. Like tasting a juicy ripe pear again for the first time. My hands caress and see her face, her neck and shoulders, her full breasts and hardening nipples, her smooth belly, her back, her round buttocks, her bushy valley and moistening engorging lips, her thighs, knees, legs, and feet.

We go to the bed and embrace in constant motion, flesh exploring and conversing with flesh. We are new lovers with the thrill and even surprise at the joy of the pleasure, connection, the sense of specialness, and of being chosen. We are also old lovers, returning to a home in each other.

As we move from the sensual to the sexual, I make extra effort to maintain the flow of energy into my heart simultaneously with the electric exchange going on with Karen. This does not diminish in any way my presence with her—in fact, it enhances it. Rather than the spiritual being separate, she is my divine lover. She is the Goddess making love with me.

Her mouth, her tongue, her breath are all the taste of the Goddess. I kiss and suckle at the round, full breasts of the Goddess made flesh.

She is also stroking and kissing me. The pleasure is exquisite, the passion like a great blaze in this vast dark universe. We are two suns coming together lighting up this boundless space.

We join in a yab/yum position with her sitting on my folded legs. We are sitting, embracing, kissing as I lift her up and down. We are all lovers who ever mated. We are God and Goddess who copulate to make the energy of life.

My ideas about myself are completely undone. I have no past, no future, only presence. I allow the great Beloved to find me. My body, mind, and being become servants of that glorious flow.

In this I am constantly working with the edge of coming. I do not want to ejaculate, and so regularly draw my sexual energies and juices back into my body. The energy races through me in inner orgasms which at times result in convulsions of pleasure and intensified body energy. I am also constantly bringing the energy into my heart center. Karen dances beautifully and sensitively with me, pausing when needed so as not to push me over this razor's edge where the sensual and mystical meet, helping me ride this wild horse without falling off into the purely sensory and releasing the juices and tensions into her (as much as she may want the pleasure of that). The intensity increases because we are able to dance on this high wire. We are out of time, beyond the temporal. Karen has a number of orgasms and I delight in her convulsive movements and high voltage energy.

After what was probably a couple of hours, we slow down and lie together, embracing and still coupled. I am not tired or exhausted. In fact I am fully awake, vibrantly energized and completely relaxed into our embrace.

When she returns to our bedroom upstairs, I am awake. The sense of the energy and consciousness continues even when I sleep. What Eros ever rejoined his Psyche with such praise and delight. I dedicate our lovemaking and ask that the gods and goddesses receive the beauty of our coupling as an offering.

The energy and glow continued through the night. The rainbow flame or flare which is continuously there is larger and more intense. The rainbow colors vary in expanse from filling all space to occupying a portion of the darkness, or to the size of a small meteor. At times last night this rainbow meteor would explode in all directions and then reform into a ball with a long tail.

During exercise this morning I still had surges of sexual energy. The Tibetan and Taoist chi kungs were especially intense. I mingled the sexual energy with the energy of the earth and heavens.

For the rest of the day, I work more with the image of Avalokiteshvara, the Bodhisattva/deity of compassion, and the other Dhyani Buddhas as wisdom figures. They give another dimension of shape and force to the practice.

One of the ideas of working with and as Avalokiteshvara is to bring to the world what are called "Bliss Bestowing Hands." In a sense this is a metaphor for the quality of presence that we bring from our work with the spiritual dimensions of being to the rest of life, to our communities, our work in the world and to nature.

Karen left for South America today. She has been a wonderful support and I feel it has deepened the bond of our marriage. I am so grateful for the way she has been during this retreat.

Working a lot with deep listening and profound silence.

Abiding in simply being. There is no self-sense—all there is, is is.

As I do Compassion tsa lung (yoga), I sense each cell in my body and particularly my heart, lungs, eyes, nose, ears, mouth, and my skin are radiating presence, light, and a quality of joy. I also sense that my cells are listening deeply to silence and to some other world vibration and rhythm.

A Poem in Honor of Last Night
    We embrace silently
    in the womb of darkest night.
    Lips unerringly find
    their moist destination.
    We give each other
    silky full body caresses
    And taste
    all the delights of lovers
    bodies unbounded, breaking free.

No vows were spoken
in that dark place,
But bonds were surely made
and anchors sunk and entwined
deep in the unseen, unknown, unknowable depths.

This skin delights at the abundance
of touch and radiates
Love with pulsing urgency
filling the universe
with the delight of Gods.

7 A Change of Heart, Surrender, and Being Worked

Sitting in the Dark

Sitting on a firm cushion, thoughts come and go

Mind remains.

Feelings arrive insistently and exit reluctantly,

Heart remains.

Inner lights and colors arise, pass through and disappear,

Darkness remains.

"I" goes

"Am" remains.

—Martin Lowenthal, Dark Retreat 2001

Day 22

Continuous consciousness throughout day and night, waking and sleeping.

The state of being continuously alert, whether asleep or awake (in the ordinary sense), took me beyond any specific form of conscious awareness to consciousness itself. This state of pure conscious awareness transcends sleeping, waking, living, and dying. A sense of unconditional home emerged not only in relation to the sensory world but in all the dimensions of being as I abide in *rigpa*. In some traditions this is called God consciousness. Some call it Clear Light, nondual awareness. Others call it the clarity and bliss of primordial awareness, and still others speak of merging with the One. For the ancient Greeks a truly conscious person was one who was taken by "Apollo's ecstasy" and was called a "skywalker" or "skydancer" (similar to the meaning of *daka* and *dakini* in the Tibetan tradition).

This state of consciousness is beyond time and space, and simultaneously I did not experience being divorced from time and space. It is inclusive of time and space, but not limited by them. Physical reality remained quite real and somehow not limiting to my sense of being and becoming.

The Clear Light of consciousness is continuous even as my body-mind had experiences, did practices, and worked in the other dimensions of my being. There was no identity with this consciousness and the identities of my activities. Eating, practicing, writing, dreaming, and sleeping were simply aspects of mind play, like clouds are aspects of weather. All dimensions of being and awareness could be there simultaneously; all hosted or included in the Clear Light of non-identified, nondual consciousness. The stability of this consciousness persisted throughout the rest of this retreat and into the period that followed.

> Wrote poetry from the time I awoke, for a couple of hours. My open natural awareness was filled with poetic images and phrases and golden threads to follow.
> Then I practiced almost continuously.
> In a strange and deep way I feel humbled. In some ways I am so

inadequate for the role of teacher and spiritual servant. Something far inside my heart is being cracked open.

Like the David Wagoner poem "Lost," when I am lost I let the darkness find me. This darker-than-night which is so immediate, embracing, and intimate and also so infinitely vast, beyond imagination.

To paraphrase Wagoner, no two moments are the same in experience.

If the freshness of each new moment is lost on you, then you are surely lost.

Stay still, you must let the moment find you.

In the evening and into the next day I wrote my own variation on Wagoner's poem "Lost."[26] I was creating a new poem using the structure of his. Unlike the poetry I wrote earlier, I decided to craft this poem. This meant that I needed to remember precisely what I had written since I could not examine early versions. I wrote many revisions which I will not include here. The process of writing the poem was also working me. I wrote revisions between practices. Each time I surrendered more and each practice became more intense. The title of my poem became "Who Are You."

Who Are You

Be still. The air you breathe and the sounds you hear
Are not confused. Who you are is Here and Now,
And you must treat it as a powerful stranger,
Must open wholeheartedly to know it and be known.
Listen. The surf of silence, it answers,
"I have made this world around you,
If you leave, you may come home again by simply attending."
No two sensations are the same to the body.
No two moments are the same in experience.
If what a sensation or a moment does is lost on you,
You are surely lost. Be still. The silence knows
Who you are. You must let it define you.

Day 23

Not sleeping much in this continuous consciousness.

Practice has been great. Having written my variation on the Wagoner poem, which I am now calling "Who Are You," I have settled into a new level. The teaching I put in my poem about letting silence define who you are—it is working me more deeply. It was a surprise to substitute the word "define" for "find" and it has taught me. What a gift from the muses.

A shift in heart postures has occurred. I feel even more at home. A deeper knowing is present, though I do not consciously understand what it is. I am more relaxed and feel complete. My practice has made the poetry possible and the writing of the poems, particularly "Who Are You," has taken me deeper and strengthened my practice.

The dissolution of self-sense in abiding has become regular as all my senses widen. My eyes widen, my ears, my listening at the back of my head, my heart center, my body and skin.

Day 24

Continuous meditation all day. Sense of being worked for hours. The setup for being worked was like opening a window or doorway to the eternal dimension and surrendering and letting a great force flow in and through me, not simply my body but my whole field of awareness (aura, room, and beyond). It feels as though my cells are open and continuous, undiminished energy is being released.

Mostly continuous sense of my heart center, third eye center, and inspiration center (or what could be called the third ear—at the back of the head).

Using integration movements and sounds at many points, with the abiding following all kinds of practices.

Lots of emphasis on listening. I find I can open powerfully to the sacred dimensions by placing my attention in either the heart center, inspiration center at the back of the head, or the third eye. Each will evoke the others. Sometimes I simply place attention in all three. I generally maintain some attention in my heart center.

Strong Compassion tsa lung/yoga. I am getting more consistent in my ability to become each wisdom deity and to see the colors filling space and to smell the fragrances. This entire retreat I have mostly used the Compassion mantra—Om Mani Padme Hum—I have it running nearly all the time, except in the abidings which are open and silent—though the mantra runs frequently on its own in the background.

Day 25

Did a very long practice session for what must have been between four and five hours. Mostly abiding and sense of being worked. It feels like my body and senses are being transformed. When I would hit a period when I tired and was getting distracted by thoughts or dream images, I kept practicing and worked until I had reopened and was being worked. Being worked requires little effort—just enough to maintain posture and attention.

Deep sense of doing all this for the benefit of the community and the world. I lose sense of my own identity and history and sense being part of something vastly larger. I am beginning to get a small understanding of the Bodhisattva tradition of working wholeheartedly to bring to the world a Bliss Bestowing Body—a presence that brings people some of the bliss world of the sacred.

Kept doing tonglen practice during bliss state of being worked.

Day 26

Awoke from conscious dreaming and sleep after a very short period feeling alert and cheery. Did ritual greeting of the day which is dark and luminous. Did morning massage to awaken my body—which I have been doing every morning. Recited poem "Love after Love" by Derek Walcott thinking particularly of his line "Feast on your life." Accessed heart space and presence.

In the shower I spontaneously began paying homage to my father. His birthday was last week and he would have been eighty-seven (he died a little over 14 years ago). Karen had once asked me what I learned from my father—the positive things.

I have done a praising of him before and I found it useful now. Here is some of that list of what I learned from him.

To love unconditionally.

To be dedicated to something you believe in.

To work hard and be disciplined about it.

To believe in people and be loyal to friends.

To have a social conscience and sense of justice.

To be warm and physically affectionate.

To treat disabilities as challenges and overcome them (he was partly crippled from polio).

To be positive in life in spite of everything (his family was poor, and he began selling newspapers on crutches when he was four years old. His father was abusive and abandoned the family of four children for years at a time).

To take delight in things and evoke it in others.

To love and support someone even when you are disappointed.

To have ideals and be romantic.

To be impractical.

To love a child unconditionally.

To have faith in your children.

To use what you have.

To have opinions and be able to defend them.

To think systematically.

To appreciate words and the search for the precise wording of a thought.

To write discourse.

To respect the human design.

To doubt rigid beliefs—religious and political.

To know I was loved—even when he was absent a lot.

To listen to music—particularly classical.

To be grateful for life and love it.

I experience the nearly continuous flow of wisdom energy in and throughout my being. It is as if the door to that dimension is open and I am being bathed, nourished, and awakened by that great force. My heart, body, and entire sense of being are vibrant and alive.

I am also resting in my nature, as Dzogchen would say, while this is being experienced. At times the resting is more the center, or rather there is no center, no thing particularly happening. It simply is—open, silent, still, and vibrant. This is impossible to express in words.

I had the sense of becoming Amitabha—the Buddha of boundless radiance, love, and clarity, and the source of generosity and compassion.

I reflect on why I have been drawn to Buddhism and have it as my core spiritual lineage. Fundamentally, Buddhism is a path that opens to all spiritual traditions, allowing me to be Jewish and to incorporate many other approaches. Perhaps I might say I am a Jewish Buddhist Plus. It is about clarity, wisdom, the human design, and service to life and all people and beings. For me, it also allows me to work with people of all religions, which is important to me in our heterogeneous society.

I am once again in the position I was last year in retreat. I could easily continue indefinitely in terms of my practice, attitude, and benefit. At the same time, there is a world of things awaiting my attention and obligations I want to honor. I also want to share my retreat in the world, although I am not sure I am fully ready and that the qualities are ripe and mature enough. I know I want to do more retreats, at least one a year.

After retreats, I keep working to have the door of my being stay open and experience the continuous flow and radiance of energy from the wisdom dimension. I can close it so easily by distractions, contractions of my heart around an issue with someone, and fears of the unexpected. I know it will require constant attention and presence to not inadvertently shut the door. The spiritual is not shy; it is we who keep shutting these divine presences out.

At times this energetic bliss body takes on weird proportions. Sometimes the right side of my face seems to get larger and larger, in fact, enormous like something in a surrealist painting. Then it returns to normal size and my forehead will expand. This is all felt, not visualized although images sometimes come to mind. Later I play with these phenomena and pick body parts to enlarge, such as my lips, my breasts, my heart, my penis, and my feet. Each area I play with responds. I then expand my senses to all space (which had happened spontaneously a number of times before). I also have the experience that my body is not only all space but all the cells are each a sun or solar system with lots of space between them.

I then expand this energy and awareness to all the people I care about, to those people in need, and to all beings.

I feel even more dedicated than before and humbled by the enormity of living up to these blessings and this mission. This is an awesome responsibility and I feel small in relation to it.

I need all the help I can get and know I need to keep surrendering to the unknown beyond me. This is the kind of gift that I must live up to and cannot ignore, or it will haunt my every movement—no escape into the mundane and trivial.

During chanting practice my voice became an expression of that creative bliss wisdom energy.

A few days ago, my practice with the bliss body would get so intense, and because I continued it during eating, daily activities, and sleeping, I would go through periods of what I might call "practice fatigue" (not in the sense of tending to go unconscious but more a physical exhaustion). Then the practice itself revived me. Now there is a sense of ease and being physically refreshed in this continuous consciousness.

Day 27

All ideas of a routine are out the window. Awoke after what must have been a couple of hours from conscious sleep and tried to go back to sleep, but was awake and energized and receiving poetry and teachings. There was a great call from the silence—"Don't go back to sleep!" So after an hour of lying there, I sat up and in my bed, seated on my pillow, and I opened. I sat there for I don't know how long, perhaps an hour or more. And unknown teachings came to me like they had in a vision quest many years ago in the Canyonlands desert of Utah.

Again, as then, I tried to report in my own head what was happening and what I was being gifted. Once again I was told, very clearly, to shut up, open, and listen. What was being planted would be known in time. The transmissions in the desert resulted in some of the Heart of Compassion teachings, in teachings on the Heart of Wisdom, in the Dedication Inquiries and Seminars, and many other teachings that have unfolded over the past ten years.

I sat with silence and stillness. At times there was nothing—no breath, no movement, no sound, no sense of sound or silence. Just Being.

Other times, the energy of bliss filled my body and all space. I sensed great energies moving through me, into my heart, into my cells.

I can understand the obsession with this divine, eternal Beloved and the longing for this bliss that is beyond pleasure. This is the grail of life.

This is the treasure of the lost city. This is Shambhala—Shangri-La. And it includes everything—the sky, the mountains, the valleys, the joys, the grief, the despair, the greed, the fear, the hunger, the cries of a baby girl in her sleep, the rage of young men lost in hopelessness, the melancholy, the celebration, the music—everything.

Here the emotions are hands for reaching out and relating—not as reactions but as wisdom-bestowing channels, not as reaching in our trying to relieve or express a feeling, but as gifts to the world that evoke awakening and peace and a sense of the great beyond.

This day continues to be guided. I have been practicing and being practiced almost continuously since beginning in bed. All day I remain awake and practicing. Seeds have been planted in my heart that I don't know, yet I feel the effects of them and their growth already.

My state seems to alternate between a still natural, Essence-state and that state combined with the vibrantly radiating bliss state.

The experience of bliss body is not so much that my body becomes all radiant space as my being and senses do.

It is evening and except for a nap this afternoon, I am still doing continuous practice and have a sense of still receiving teachings. Today is such an unplanned blessing, a kind of climax for the retreat.

Day 28

Sensing, looking deeply and listening into the infinite vastness of still, silent heart space. Experiencing this simultaneously with radiance—vast, infinite, vibrant space.

Awoke from conscious sleep again after a very short sleep and was already practicing. The energy was pulsing. I thought of trying to go back to sleep and the voice of some presence spoke in my head and said, "You've been asleep most of your life. Don't go back to sleep now that you are awake."

So I practiced and did special preparation for coming out of the dark, transitioning from seeing only inner lights and lights from the sacred dimensions of being into external light of the world.

Before the sound of birds at dawn, I did the integration practice. I first integrated movement with the bliss state and natural mind, then sound using chanting, then movement and sound, and then I removed the curtains and window insert and integrated the light of external night.

I then meditated with the light of night for a while and practiced as I made the adjustment. All through these last few days I have both practiced and been practiced.

After some time I left the retreat space and went into the main part of the house. I put on a heavy jacket, shoes, and gloves and went into the refreshing, cold (actually below-freezing) night and walked in the woods.

A half moon was barely visible through the cloudy sky. My eyesight was great for night vision. A path that would have been dark to me normally was now quite visible. Walking was strange. I had forgotten that, although I exercised every day, I had not really walked anywhere or gone up or down an incline for a month. Also, the adjustment to lights seems to affect the sense of balance.

When I returned to the house, I went into the main meditation hall and practiced with the thankas (sacred Tibetan paintings) and sacred statues in the room. The colors of the paintings are outstanding; they literally stand out from the surface of each thanka. The figures come alive with a kind of pulsing. I worked particularly with Avalokiteshvara and Manjushri—the Bodhisattvas or deities of compassion and wisdom. My entire being would connect to them and they not only filled my heart space, but I became them. I also worked with Tapretza (the Bön version of Samantabajra), the deity of the pure nature of mind—Essence. That was also very powerful.

I practiced there for a couple of hours. When I did simple abiding and hosting, I found that as my eyes maintained a soft gaze and no focus, I would often see lights that were much brighter than the lamps or daylight. I was able to see the deeper spiritual lights.

Arrington, a student who has been staying in the house and been my main support person since Karen left, came in and joined me for the last part and we ended with a co-meditation.

It is now eight A.M. and I have returned to the retreat room to practice in here in the light for today.

Part III
A Framework for
Understanding the Teachings

Dharmakaya is the total dimension of existence, without any exclusion.
Thus it corresponds to the essence, the ineffable and immeasurable
condition beyond all the concepts and limits of dualism.

—Namkhai Norbu

1 Purpose of Spiritual Work

The basic purpose of the teachings and practices is to reveal the hidden wisdom base in confused reactions and make that hidden nature manifest. By recognizing and cultivating the inherent wisdom of our nature, we shift our ground of being from distress to creativity, disturbance to balance, and suffering to well-being. We use the dynamics of aliveness to align our body, mind, and heart, becoming a beneficial presence in the world.

In a sense we come home to our authentic nature which is simultaneously at home in the Essence of all being, in our radiant wisdom potential, in the world of nature, and in the community of people, including those in need.

In approaching teachings about the recognition of the nature of all reality, it is helpful to have a way of understanding that reality. This understanding can inform our practice and place our experiences in some overall context. It is not as if the understanding were the key to realization in spiritual work, for it is not. The key is in our own open, wholehearted efforts that create the conditions for recognition to arise, yet an understanding can assist our alignment of the mind with the practices.

2 Dimensions of Being

There are many ways of describing the nature of being, probably as many as there are spiritual traditions. My own experience is that there are many dimensions of being and many modes of awareness, and at the same time, there is fundamentally only what is; there is only one true nature, Essence, one God.

Dharma is a term derived from the Sanskrit *dhri* (to hold) and is used to refer to many things, such as the teachings, all phenomena, the path, nirvana, as well as life. Namkhai Norbu says that "Dharma means existence"; in other words, being. He also points out that the three *kayas*—nirmanakaya, sambhogakaya, and dharmakaya, which he refers to as "bodies" or "dimensions"—are not levels. They are dimensions of the whole, "both material and immaterial, in which we find ourselves."

We can identify many dimensions of being, or a multiplicity of layers to existence, some of them evident, but most hidden. These dimensions are not a hierarchy or progression in the sense that any are

109

necessarily more important than others or come into being in some sequence. Reality simply is. It includes all dimensions simultaneously and each is inseparable from the others.

To simplify, we will refer to three primary dimensions that correspond to the three kayas—the sensory, the subtle, and Essence.

The sensory is a continuum (variously referred to as form, the physical, the body, earth, gross body, manifestation, nirmanakaya) from matter through the body, to the feelings, to the mental and emotional processes. The latter create both identity and relationship, and are at the edge of the subtle continuum.

The subtle (variously called the formative, soul, subtle mind, archetypical or essence of the human, subtle body, energetic, the splendor or delight body, indestructible aspect of our own being, sambhogakaya) continuum goes from self-sense of presence through witness to subtle awareness and energy, the intuitive, the creative, sacred value, and the wisdom qualities and energies.

The Essence (Fundamental Nature of all Being, Nature of Mind, the Divine, Transcendent and Immanent God, Spirit, Ein Sof, Godhead, Ultimate Nature, Dharmakaya) simply is. It is not definable. It is both transcendent and immanent; everything in all dimensions arises out of and is made up of Essence. Experientially, its open (empty) nature is reflected in the transience of all phenomena and experiences, and its hosting nature means everything is included; nothing arises outside of it. It is the unconditional space within which existence arises and is hosted.

3 Three Aspects of Being: Awareness, Energy, and Relationship

There are three aspects to all being. All that exists arises in space (awareness), manifests (activity/energy), and is distinguished from and in relationship to everything else that manifests (relationship).

When we engage in practice, we consciously work with one or more of these three aspects and seek to realize the enlightened quality of each. For example, in awareness practices we aim at wisdom. In working with energy the aim is radiance, and relating directly to manifest reality develops presence.

Awareness

Awareness is the sensing, knowing, or apprehension of something, even if it is not conscious. We obviously have an awareness of the content of our thoughts, and this could be called a surface awareness. Our bodies are constantly making physical adjustments to light, temperature, and the surfaces on which we are sitting, standing, or lying. This is a body awareness. We may not notice those elements, yet they operate anyway. We also have mental and emotional awarenesses which make up aspects of the body/mind system. Then we have other awarenesses which make up our being and self-sense, but which may not be noticed until we develop the ability to include them. These make up the subtle dimensions and include the subtle energetic, the open witness, and the various wisdom awarenesses. Pure awareness corresponds to Essence. Together, these make up the dimensions or modes of awareness. Each modality has its own way of knowing, its own internal structure, its own relationship to the self-system, to the world, and to Essence.

A metaphor for these dimensions or worlds of awareness might be a solar system. From the viewpoint of everyday consciousness, we are a planet around which everything else seems to revolve. During the day we may get glimpses of a sun (our wisdom nature), but the clouds often obscure it. At night we have no sense of the sun except by reflection off the moon. Likewise, our identities seem to make us special, and this consciousness appears to be the most important.

From the point of view of the sun (our wisdom nature), the planets are small and all contained by the field of energy of the sun. There are many planets which revolve around the sun, not simply the planet of surface thoughts and feelings. The planet of sensations is larger and has a wider, more encompassing orbit. The world of the energy of manifestation is larger and wider still. The world of witness is even larger and its orbit is so wide it encompasses the material, mental, and emotional worlds. The entire system, including the sun, is hosted in space, the awareness within which everything arises. This is the transcendent mode of awareness beyond knowing and not knowing, beyond distinction, and beyond all concepts.

Through our practice we seek to recognize the less obvious awarenesses and particularly pure awareness, also known as rigpa. Based on our recognition we expand our conscious attention to include the multiplicity of dimensions of awareness and have them inform and shape our way of being in the world to reflect their basic wisdom nature.

Energy

Energy is the activity of being and each dimension of being has its own energy, its own activity. The types of energies are numerous, ranging from those of the physical dimension which produce results, and many of which can be measured by our senses, to those of the subtle dimensions that represent activities corresponding to the mythic and wisdom modes of awareness.

These are all expressions of the activity of Essence. All other dimensions and phenomena are simply aspects or modifications of that fundamental activity or energy.

The word energy comes from the Greek *energeia,* meaning "active." It also means the "capacity of acting, operating or producing an effect, whether exerted or not." In the teachings, we generally use both of these meanings of energy—as activity and the capacity or potential for activity.

Energy is both formative and form, is both elemental (basic) and constantly transforming, is unseen and can manifest, is infinite and measurable, and can be latent or active. Because everything that exists is activity—whether the activity of atoms, of light and sound, or thoughts and feelings—energy as activity is both a process and a result, a dynamic and material form. It is the actor, action, and result of action. It is the creative impulse, the creative imagination, the creator, the act of creating, and the creation. It is all five, in various degrees of action and form.

In our practice, the energetic vitalizes the awareness and makes it possible for wisdom to become embodied. We harmonize the elemental energies in healing and cultivate the wisdom energies in transforming our body of habits.

Relationship

Everything that exists is always in relation to everything else that exists. Thich Nhat Hanh calls this interbeing. This inherent interconnection pervades all aspects of our experience, even when we feel alone. Our impulse to make meaning is a way of relating and connecting and is a manifestation of the interrelated nature of all being.

The sense of longing for belonging arises from the fixation of our attention on the superficial or material dimension, of our being in a kind of amnesia about the deeper dimensions of life and interbeing. Instead of experiencing others as an expression of connectedness, we focus on our sense of separation, need, and tension. We hope to find a home where we belong and can rest. With clarity we know our natural connection and can relate directly through our presence.

The importance of relationship can be seen in the tantric art of the vedic and Tibetan traditions. We find images of the primordial god and goddess in loving embrace and sexual congress. One represents openness and the other radiance, formlessness and form, awareness and energy, Essence and manifestation. While there are two figures, representing two of the aspects of reality, they are always in relationship, always relating in the ecstatic and inseparable embrace of love. One figure by itself calls our attention to that aspect of existence, but the true nature of things is only fully realized in the union of the two figures, the experience of direct relationship.

Emotions are often misunderstood as part of the spiritual path in the Buddhist traditions. The so-called afflictive emotions such as anger, fear, and sadness are only one subset of the larger set of emotional phenomena. The emotions are the activity of relating, which involves perception, recognition, meaning, expression, and connection. They are an integral part of life, just as sensations, imagination, and energies are and can be used to either enhance our spiritual development or diminish it. The activity of the emotional is how we conventionally know something is true, how we connect to our own physical and psychological states, how we relate to others, and how we relate to the world, to life, and to the sacred. The emotions are what motivate us, get us involved on a path, keep us going, and connect us to the teachings, our teachers, and our community.

For example, the practice of guru yoga involves connecting with a teacher and the lineage of teachers and seeing them in all their wisdom qualities as a conduit to the essence of wisdom itself. The living, breathing nature of teachers allows us to relate to wisdom beyond any concepts we may have and experience the wisdom dimension as manifesting in our form.

The teacher can open our hearts to qualities of wisdom and transmit some of the energetic juices that activate them in our being. Recalling and invoking the teachers connects us to that wisdom dimension of being which awakens our hearts and prepares us to engage wholeheartedly in practice with the sense of loving support of the teachers.

In guru yoga, to be inspired by the vision and example of teachers and deities, and to allow ourselves to dissolve and be reformed by that inspiration, love, and devotion, is the blessing and method of this practice. This is my essential experience of guru yoga. In it, I hold my teachers and wisdom beings and lineage in my heart. I feel their love, wisdom, and encouragement filling my heart, my body, and my entire being.

In the practice I make myself a carrier of their wisdom in the world and become responsible for their legacy. Guru yoga accesses my love, my desire to grow, my dedication, and my sense of being a part of a larger story through time.

In tantric deity practices, we first connect to the deity and then transform ourselves into the deity, working to feel and relate as the deity does. Our ability to connect directly and feel intensely deepens the impact of the practice on our bodies and being.

Ritual is another practice that uses our capacity to relate. The word ritual comes from *ritus*, Latin meaning "to fit together." Ritual weaves the fragments of our lives into a vital fabric of meaning, individually and collectively. Ritual takes us beyond our daily pressures and self-concerns into a larger world of myth, spirits, and wisdom. Ritual is action that connects us and expresses our relationship to both the seen and unseen worlds, including the sacred wisdom qualities and energies (which are often called "beings").

Sacred rituals comprise a form of celebrational practice. They ceremonially praise, supplicate, evoke, invoke, and activate the energies and qualities of the spiritual dimensions. They align us with those dimensions to give direction to our work, our relationships, and our growth.

4 Reactive Habit Body/Samsaric Mind of Confusion

Although we would like to feel alive and at home in all aspects of life—physical, emotional, mental, and spiritual—we tend to treat the world as a barrier and a problem. In fact, the problem is not the world; it is our own habits of thinking and feeling, likes and dislikes, which are distracting, confusing, and reactive. In our habitual ways of being and doing, we often experience life as a prison in which we are doing time trying to avoid fears, satisfy longings, and struggle with confusion and boredom.

According to Buddhist theory, the basic causes of ordinary reactive experience are cognitive in origin. We live in a reality made up of mental constructs of perceptions, assumptions, beliefs, processes, and identities that grow out of our reactions to life and do not reflect reality, things as they are.

This personally constructed reality makes up our reactive habit body, the mental, emotional, and physical habits which we develop over the course of this life (and according to traditional Buddhism, which we have also accumulated from past lives in the form of tendencies). This habit body both creates and is itself created by our fundamental attitudes or postures of the heart, what the Tibetans call "view."

Postures of the Heart

Postures of the Heart refers to our basic attitudes, self-images, compelling concerns, and ways of relating to the world. It includes the stance we take toward ourselves, others, and the world. This affects our perceptions, our mental processes, our feelings, and the way we physically organize ourselves.

Our identifications and our habitual reactions around those identities shape our heart postures toward life and our sense of reality. These postures include who we unconsciously think we are and what we feel compelled to accept as true about life. Our heart postures are so powerful that they constantly orient and direct us. Even in the face of apparent contradiction, we continue to seek evidence to support our core beliefs until our experience conforms to that reality.

The body of habits formed in early life were based on the limited cognitive capacity and the needs of a child, and must be outgrown and reformulated if we are to mature and move through the stages and passages of life. Buddhism is based on the view that ego identities are mistaken ideas about who we are, and that each of us can discover the truth. Spiritual teachings work from the premise that a core of wisdom and beneficial intention is basic to the human design and that we can become free of our reactive structures. This core is not adopted or imposed; rather, it is discovered and nurtured as part of our growth and maturation. The tradition of working with this core has been at the heart of the wisdom and spiritual traditions for thousands of years.

Freedom from Being Hostage to Ourselves

The nature of freedom is that it is relative to something else. We can experience freedom from constraints and limitation, freedom to be and act, and freedom to live on behalf of others. The clearest statement about the nature of our condition was given decades ago at a Passover ceremonial meal by my son Micah, who was five years old at the time. As I was explaining the meaning of the bitter herbs in the Jewish tradition that remind us of the bitterness of slavery, he said, "It seems to me that we are all really slaves to ourselves."

This process of freeing ourselves from reactive mental, emotional, and physical habits which keep us hostage to our fears, wants, longings, and hopes is at the core of reorienting and retraining ourselves. We want

• freedom from Confusion to have the freedom of Clarity,

• freedom from Alienation to be free in the sense of Home,

• freedom from Contraction to be free to Grow,

• freedom from Pretension and Reaction to have Poise and Choice,

• freedom from Fear to act from Wisdom and Generosity,

• freedom from Reactive Self-Concern to becoming an Active Presence with and for others and the world.

Our wisdom presence is an expression of freedom. We are free when we act in accordance with our wisdom, free to be authentic, natural, and beneficial without qualification.

5 Wisdom Nature

Wisdom, as a way of being and a core knowing about life and the nature of reality, is both a result of spiritual practice and a means toward full realization of our sacred nature. Wisdom has many facets, like a diamond, in which, when the light of attention shines through its fundamentally clear, crystalline nature, various colors are seen, each a quality of wisdom and an energy of being.

Wisdom also includes the essence or pure formative intelligence that informs manifestation. Each of these formative wisdom qualities can be sensed as an energetic presence when we are open and attentive enough to the subtle dimensions of awareness. These energetic presences can be seen as lights, listened to as vibrations, smelled as fragrances, and felt as subtle energies of consciousness.

True clarity includes both profound wisdom, the perception of the nature of being, and the qualities of wisdom such as love, compassion, equanimity, generosity, authenticity, and hosting, all of which flow from profound wisdom.

Love is one of the qualities most universally accepted as a central wisdom quality. Love in a spiritual sense is a way of perceiving, praising, and relating to life. In Buddhism it is called *maitri* (in Sanskrit, *metta* in Pali), in Judaism it is *hesed,* and it is living in the path of Jesus' love in the Christian tradition. It is often called "loving kindness" and "compassion" and can refer to the authentic desire that others enjoy happiness. It is spontaneous, natural, and unqualified. This form of love has an emotional component but arises from a wisdom clarity which is unconditional and perceives the wisdom nature of all beings. This is a heart posture that is cultivated through formal practice and by service in the world. It is a quality of being that must begin at home with oneself and those dear to us. Then we can apply it in an ever-widening circle to all people, all beings, and all creation.

6 Coming Home

One of our principal longings is to feel and to be an intimate part of some whole, to experience belonging. This longing is to be simply who we are, without reservation or condition. This sense of belonging is often called "home."

When we come home, we rest in our own nature and experience the intimacy of all life. Experience is direct. There is no separation between the experience, what is experienced, and the witnessing self. As we learn to abide in this nature with wonder and gratitude, the unknown, remote, and seemingly threatening aspects of all worlds reveal their hidden vitality and affinity to us. Our thoughts, images, and feelings then simply give expression and articulation to this fundamental relationship that embraces humanity, all living beings, nature, and divinity as one. In the heart of wisdom there is no real division between me and you, here and there, time and eternity, or the human and the divine. Everywhere is home. Nowhere is home. Our hosting Essence nature welcomes, includes, and supports everything as being home.

The Four Homes

Aligning ourselves with the dimensions of being means that we rest in each dimension in a natural way and experience the richness, intimacy, and love of all life. Each dimension of being has a different quality of home. We could posit that there are four homes:

• Home in Being (Essence, the Sacred Universal beyond time and space)

• Home for Wisdom (Subtle, the Sacred Universal in its formative aspect)

• Home in the World (Sensory, the Material World of nature, community, and life forces)

• Home for Those in Need (Manifesting Compassion as the union of all elements and homes through service)

At the fundamental level, the most pervasive sense of home comes when we relax our attention in the open dimension of being of Essence. The experience of a home in being arises spontaneously when we have created the appropriate inner conditions. The home for wisdom is both something that arises spontaneously as insight and is cultivated in the sense of retraining the body/mind to manifest the qualities of wisdom that we discover. Our home in the world grows out of our relationships to other people, to our community, to nature, and to the visible and invisible forces that sustain and enrich life. The home for those in need is the path of service that combines the sacred qualities of awareness and energy from the other three homes.

7 Meditation

The purpose of meditation is to bring us home to the realization of our authentic unitive nature—being totally open, boundlessly radiant, and always presencing. This nature is the fundamental awareness out of which everything arises and passes through, and into which it disappears. It underlies the whole of life and death—of body, mind, and soul, all that exists, all possibilities. The basis of meditation is experience, recognition, and cultivation.

Meditation is a path which is rooted in the ground of a vision of the human design and possibility. This path of spiritual practice is a process of growth which initially involves relaxing the body and the mind, training the mind to stabilize attention, training the will, witnessing and hosting whatever arises, cultivating wisdom qualities and training the body/mind to manifest those qualities, and to rest in our essential nature.

8 Training Attention and Mindfulness

Meditation involves the conscious placement and maintenance of attention. The capacity for intentionally using attention is one of the precious gifts of life. Attention is the ability to direct the mind and apply the range of energies of our being. Attention is the lens which brings all things into view. It is a beacon that reveals the nearest and farthest reaches of the inner world and brings the outer world into intimate relationship with us.

We can attend to things, thoughts, feelings, witnessing, and/or ways of being. Our attention can be totally taken up with our mental commentary on how to apply this book on the surface dimension of awareness. Or we can place our attention in other dimensions of awareness such as the sensations in our hands; or sounds in the room; or the meaning of this passage; the feelings we are having as we read; witnessing all those sensations, sounds, thoughts, and feelings, and/or we can host the various awarenesses, including some or all of them.

As we go deeper into the sacred dimensions, the task requires an unusual commitment to training our attention. The movement of attention is a bit like traveling. We can be a tourist and visit each dimension of being, getting a sense of the awareness and the landscape of that dimension. We visit the sacred like we would Paris or the Grand Canyon or the temples at Angkor Wat. We see the beauty and outstanding surface features, but we have little or no understanding of what it would be like to live there.

To become a resident, we have to learn new ways of perceiving, new ways of relating, different values, and a changed sense of ourselves and our habits. As is the case with integrating another culture, this takes time and practice. It requires becoming open and fresh. It also requires that we be fully engaged in the experiences of our lives and awake enough so that we are actively authentic rather than unconsciously reactive.

Mindfulness is the English translation of the Pali word *sati*. In the experience of mindfulness we are consciously aware and present in the moment. Mindfulness keeps us present, allows us to clearly see things as they are, shows the difference between clear perception and conceptual ideas, and leads us to the perception of the true nature of all phenomena.

Mindfulness is both a goal and the means to that goal. We achieve full mindfulness, resting in the nature of our mind, by being increasingly mindful. In a sense, mindfulness is the simultaneous practice of concentration, the ability to stabilize the mind in a state without distraction, and decentration, the ability to open attention to whatever is arising.

From a developmental perspective, we can distinguish three stages of mindfulness—effortful, natural, and stable. We initially apply effort to attend consciously. With practice, our natural awake quality begins to emerge, but it tends to come and go and we move back and forth between effortful and natural mindfulness. Eventually, being naturally awake becomes stable and we can abide and operate from within that state.

In this progression we begin by intentionally placing our attention in a witness dimension of awareness, becoming aware of the surface layers of awareness and the sensory dimension of being. Since our habitual way of thinking, feeling, and acting is usually a captive of the surface level and the sensory, material world, it takes applied effort to keep some of our attention in a subtle, more consciously aware dimension. This awake, subtle dimension is always present, but we do not notice it most of the time because our mind is conditioned to attend almost exclusively to the sensory.

As our meditation practice develops and our capacity for multiple attention and presence grows, the subtle, awake dimension which is always present more naturally arises in our attention. As our practice matures, this mindfulness is present more continuously and our sense of presence becomes stable.

This mindfulness includes the capacity to openly witness exactly what is occurring in the way a mirror reflects images without distortion, comment, like, or dislike. It is a pure awareness beyond thinking and conceptualization. It is alert, bare attention.

Intimate witnessing is the direct, immediate quality of being present in the moment. This witnessing initially involves the activity of noticing whatever is occurring in life. Over time we realize that witnessing is an aspect of being present and can include mental noticing, but not necessarily. This capacity for witnessing is an aspect of our human design as a wisdom being.

The intimate witness is always awake. This sacred dimension of awareness is present at all times and knows each experience intimately. It is intimate and involved, but unattached, making no judgments and bringing no commentary or agenda. Like a mirror which reflects all images without having the qualities of any image, so the intimate witness remains open without being disturbed by changes in our lives. Our attention can be disturbed, but the witness awareness persists. The witness aspect does not need to "let go" because it is never attached. It can be distinguished as a dimension of awareness but it is not separate.

The witness we are discussing here is not the "numb observer" which is disassociated, remote, and experiences events as though they are happening to someone else. The numb observer is distant and unfeeling and withdraws the energy of aliveness from situations. Everything is reduced to information, rather than energetic engagement and reciprocal flow.

This engagement is not to be confused with immersed and entangled attitudes of the personality, where the world is whatever you are feeling and doing. The attachment to personality preoccupies our attention with reactive thoughts and feelings. The reactive observer judges, feels needy, is haunted by longing, feels diminished or defeated by painful experience, and/or wants to merge with pleasurable experiences.

To the intimate witness, all phenomena are a play of light and energy within limitless space. The intimate witness brings the awake quality to the sense of presence in the moment and thus is transcending and transformative. When we newly discover intimate witnessing, experience offers the opportunity of the sacred. In developed intimate witnessing, all experience is sacred—an expression and celebration of the wisdom nature of all being.

In other words, we do not renounce sensory life, the life of the body, emotions, and mind, but rather notice how we make ourselves unhappy and get stuck in reactive habits. By self-investigation we reveal not only the structure and nature of those habits of mind, but also the deeper nature or context within which all these phenomena arise. We also discover how the process of thinking and feeling arises, operates, and dissolves.

Hosting

The attention of witnessing brings a sense of inclusion, of hosting, to our sense of presence. It does not require the mental act of noticing, although that may be included. The key is bringing a sense of hosting presence which opens us to the vastness of the sacred world.

9 Recognition and Dzogchen

We can relax into a more natural state at this very moment and sense it as fresh, vivid, and unspoiled. Nothing is needed and nothing needs to be taken away. Even the weight of our confusion and pain can become light when we penetrate the shield of our hopes and fears and reach the energy of our direct experience. The awareness in this moment is open, luminous, and whole, rather than clouded by expectation, shaded by disappointment, and fragmented by resistance.

The principle of Dzogchen is the fundamental open nature of being. This essential and immanent nature is always true and can be recognized at any time in any situation. We do practices to enable us to recognize the nature of mind, but it is possible for this recognition to occur by transmission from a teacher, in the course of life, and from all varieties of activities and situations.

The key is not simply the glimpse of recognition but sustaining attention in that clarity. This clarity can be maintained along with other dimensions of awareness if we train ourselves for that. It can be a foundation for other work such as tantra, transformative work in the world, and creating an environment of wisdom, love, peace, and beauty.

10 Training to Embody Wisdom—The Inner Alchemy of Tantra

All experience can be used as nourishment for spiritual growth by the intentional use of attention to access awareness, subtle energies, compassion, and authenticity. Although there is a popular notion that tantra is sexual practice, the principle of tantra is not about sex, yet it does not exclude sex. It is about transformation of thoughts, emotions, the body, and everyday experiences. It is about turning the lead of the ordinary into the gold of wisdom.

Tantra is spiritual alchemy that creates a wisdom body. Because it uses the physical body, the mind, and experience, it includes powerful impulses and energies. The sexual is one of our creative and generative capacities as human beings. So tantra is not generally or even specifically about sex, but includes the sensual and sexual as one of the most powerful forces in the human design. Tantric love can induce an open state beyond concepts that is nondual. In addition it can transform an emotional energy into love as a ground of being, an unconditional wisdom state.

Tibetan teachings use the term tantra to refer both to esoteric texts which contain the teachings and to the systems of meditation practice based on those esoteric texts that train the practitioner for cognitive transformation using ritual, visualization, sound, symbols, and often movement. In the tantric system, the practitioner is conceived in terms of subtle energies, called *lung* or winds, that travel through channels, *tsa,* and that are concentrated in certain areas called *chakras.* The most important channels in tantra are a central (core) channel, which is roughly contiguous with the spine, and a left and right channel.

From a tantric point of view, consciousnesses ride the winds that carry them throughout the body. Consciousness without wind cannot function and wind without consciousness is aimless. They function together, with winds providing movement and aliveness and consciousness providing direction and quality. This intimate relationship is used by meditators to create the conditions for particular kinds of consciousness and states of being.

In Tibetan teachings and practices most tantra involves practices with deities of wisdom. In the deity practices we first call upon the wisdom deity for support, then sense our connection, receive the transmission of wisdom energy from the deity in our chakras, particularly the heart, and into our central channel, and eventually merge into the quality and energy of wisdom as the deity. In this merging we experience a bliss that is grounded in equanimity. This way of being is a form of ecstasy.

Ecstasy

As we progress in combining our attention, hosting presence, and conscious engagement, the energies of wisdom and creation arise out of the moment. This union of deity and self, of love and desire, of action with deep harmony, of energy and openness gives rise to a quality of ecstasy.

This ecstasy of being is not a concept or an emotion. It is not something explosive or excited. It is an inner fire that is radiant and sweet. All of us have experienced moments of ecstasy, listening to music, gazing at the sunset, viewing the vastness of the Grand Canyon, or the simple blissful awe of a birth. In these moments we dissolve into the pure love of life, resting in pure being with an open heart.

When we experience this ecstasy in our practice, we develop an attitude that we will not settle for anything less in life. The beauty of it invites us and the energy propels us. However, we must build ourselves as a container for it. Unless the body/mind and attention are trained, the energy can lead to emotional excitation, mental grandiosity, and a kind of manic obsessiveness, that eventually leads to a crash and depression.

Having the capacity to work with the flow of ecstatic aliveness, we make our lives a work of art, with every breath another stroke of color, every word a line, every action a form, and every encounter another painting. We transform the canvas of the world into a landscape of rich colors and multiple perspectives—into a vibrant portrait of wisdom.

To develop sacred wisdom and authentic spiritual presence requires practice. Only through spiritual practice can we sustain the direct experience of living Reality. Only through spiritual work can we create the conditions for clarity, harmonize the elements and dimensions of our being, recognize our true wisdom nature, and cultivate wisdom qualities in the transformation of the reactive habit body into the embodiment of wisdom. This is not simply having a new understanding of ourselves and the world; it involves a transformation of our consciousness and the nature of understanding itself.

Part IV
Bön Teachings on Dark Retreat

If we remain in the darkness, we will discover the radiance of wisdom.
If we practice and become familiar with that, we will quickly attain
Buddhahood. Here posture and breathing are linked with the essence
of the light of wisdom. The wisdom eye opens and we will be able to
see everything in the three worlds. This is why we do the dark retreat.

—Shardze Rinpoche

My knowledge and understanding of dark retreats comes almost
entirely from experience and that is what much of this book is based
upon. I began doing dark retreats in 1994 under the guidance and oral
instructions of the Tibetan teacher Tenzin Wangyal Rinpoche. These
teachings were supplemented by direct personal teachings in interviews
with Lopon Tenzin Namdak during his annual trips to the United States.
Few of the Tibetan teachings on this subject are available in English.

Tenzin Wangyal has a short section on his own dark retreat in his
book *Wonders of the Natural Mind*. Speaking of his seven-week dark
retreat while he was an adolescent, Tenzin Wangyal wrote, "My dark
retreat was very successful and brought about a great change in my

personality. . . . The first day I slept quite a lot; but already the second day was much better, and every day there was an improvement in my experience of the practice and my capacity to remain in the dark. It was a great experience in terms of being in contact with myself. . . . After the first week, my subjective sensation of time changed, and I lost all sense of time, so that seven days felt like two. . . . Starting from the second week, I started to have many visions of rays of light, flashes of *thigles,* rainbows, and different symbols. After the second week, the first forms resembling concrete reality started to appear. . . . Sometimes the visions changed from one form to another. . . . Almost at the end of my retreat I experienced my clarity increasing greatly. . . . Through the retreat I purified many things in myself and developed my practice and clarity. . . . After my retreat, I became so calm and quiet that my mother said that all my sisters should do a dark retreat!"[27]

1 Dzogchen

Dzogchen is the Tibetan practice of the nature of mind. Dzogchen works with the essence of all being and that which is beyond everything. It is often referred to as the direct path of liberation in which we are able to recognize the open nature of experience. We see each experience exactly as it is, without treating it as having power of its own or requiring any response. We are free to experience whatever arises and free from the experience. We do not become attached or try to own it, we are not owned by it, and there is nothing we need to do about it.

In Dzogchen, all the phenomena of experience and all the cognitive structures of ordinary mind have their base in the nature of mind, which is the base of all reality. A fundamental reality of being is awareness itself, which is beyond all dimensions and types of awareness. The nature of this reality of pure awareness is rigpa, our open, aware, and ever-present nature.

While our practice initially calms and stabilizes the mind, the deeper spiritual purpose of meditation is living continuously with the presence of the fundamental state of pure open, hosting awareness. The practice at this point is a form of contemplation that is aimed at the instant presence of pure awareness, or rigpa. In contemplation, we relax completely so that all tensions, reactive habits, and distractions effortlessly release.

Rigpa as a verb means to know or be aware. While the word has many meanings, in Dzogchen it refers to a natural awareness that is beyond all forms and is intrinsically open, inclusive, radiant, spontaneous, and immanent. The experience of the totally open, transcendent nature of pure being is wonderfully alive, alert, radiant, and ecstatic. In this experience of rigpa, the world arises as a display of beauty and love, the radiant manifesting quality of Reality.

2 The Five Elements and Dark Retreat

In the Tibetan traditions, the elements play a critical role in the generation, sustaining, dissolving, and destruction of the physical universe. At the same time these natural elements also represent more fundamental aspects of the "primordial energy of existence." Thus what is true at the universal level also applies to individuals: the elemental processes "create the body, mind, and personality. . . . And during the whole of life, the individual's relationship to the elements determines the quality of experience."[28]

In his teachings of the "*Nyam Gyu,* The Experiential Transmission of Drugyalwa Yndrung" in Boston, Tenzin Wangyal explained how to set up a dark retreat, the body postures that are used to clarify, balance, and activate the energy channels to "move the internal lights and visions and help to bring them out"; the connections between the position and gaze of the eyes and the experiences of the lights of the subtle channels; the qualities of resting the mind in the natural state; and the application of subtle energy to reveal the pure aspect of the mind.

In the *Nyam Gyu* teachings, Tenzin Wangyal pointed out that when we create the right conditions, lights and visions will naturally arise in the dark. He described how various kinds of experience arise from the activities and balance of the elements of earth, fire, wind, water, and space. After describing the fruits and results of practice in the dark, he advised "neither being swayed by those joyful experiences, nor being depressed when they are not rising. Do not expect anything!"

In the Bön system, at the physical level the energetic qualities of the five elements—earth, water, fire, air, and space—are understood as grounded stability, peaceful flow, creativity, caring flexibility, and openness. At this level, the elemental energies affect our bodies and our minds, and are considered to be the primary basis for physical and mental health and well-being.

In dark retreat, many visual phenomena can arise. Some of the colors and shapes that arise in our minds can be seen in dark space and are indicative of the degree of balance in our elements. "The internal processes of the elemental energies are reflected out, into the black room, and are reflected back to the practitioner as visions and experiences."[29] One of the retreat practices involves using five body postures and gazes to open particular channels associated with each of the five elements. When practiced while abiding in rigpa, these become "gates for the energies that allow the elemental energies to manifest externally."[30] One of the purposes for these practices is to "connect with the pure essence of the elements, the five pure lights, and the visions are the signs that the process is occurring. The visions are not the point of the practice, the internal changes are, but the visions are a way to check on the progress."[31]

As the elements manifest in the dark, the Tibetan teachings state that specific colors and shapes will tend to arise. For example, white lights and half-moon shapes are indicative of space. Red lights and triangle shapes indicate fire. Yellow squares are associated with earth. Green lights and rectangles indicate air. And circular blue lights are water. They may appear as fragments for brief periods at early stages, and, as we become more stable in our attention, they become whole and can remain for lengthier periods.

When we are out of balance, the elements are often experienced as reactive emotions such as fear and anger that hold us in their grip. As we become more stable and balanced, the elements appear as lights, and even patterns of light, and then they dissolve into a Clear Light of pure being.

3 Teachings of Lopon Tenzin Namdak

Lopon Tenzin Namdak, commenting in response to what I shared about my initial retreats, made distinctions between personal dark retreats, dark retreats oriented around the recognition of the Clear Light of the natural state, and dark retreats that prepared the practitioner for the six bardo states that follow death. I incorporated and adapted some of those teachings in later, more extended retreats, including the month-long retreat that is the core of this book.

Many of these teachings about dark retreats are included in a booklet published by the Bönpo Translation Project—*The Instructions of Shardza Rinpoche for the Practice of Vision and The Dark Retreat* from the *rDzogs-chen sku-gsum rangshar,* according to the oral commentary of Lopon Tenzin Namdak, transcribed and edited by Vajranatha (John Myrdhin Reynolds). In this work, Lopon Tenzin Namdak explains the basic principles of Dzogchen and the role of visions and dark retreats in the Bön practice. He describes the teachings of Shardze Rinpoche concerning dark retreats.

Shardze Rinpoche on Dark Retreat

Shardze Rinpoche's text covers much of the philosophy and many of the vision practices of Dzogchen, as well as the Tibetan view of these retreats.

For Tibetan Buddhist and Bön practitioners, the stability of the natural state (rigpa) is one of the most important conditions to achieve and to use in dark retreat. With the base of the natural state, primordial awareness arises that is an immediate intuition of reality that is "nondual in character." Where the Natural State is "like the sun in the clear open sky," primordial awareness is "like the rays of the sun that illuminate everything in the world."[32] By training ourselves in recognizing and abiding in the Natural State, we have the possibility of recognizing the Clear Light. These are all seen with the eye of rigpa, the eye of fundamental clarity. According to the Tibetan Buddhist and Bön traditions, the final outcome of these practices is the attainment of the "rainbow body," a body of pure light of supreme Buddhahood.

The text gives three principal types of instruction. The first concerns how to prepare for a dark retreat. The preparation involves knowledge of the teachings, introduction to the natural state by a master, instructions of a teacher, a suitable location, and a support system.

The second deals with the various kinds of distractions and disturbances that interrupt our dark retreat practice or become obstacles to abiding in the "natural state." The outer disturbances consist of human and non-human beings. Inner disturbances include illness and imbalances of the "humors" (energies). There are also distractions and obstacles that are related to the experiences that arise in meditation that are called "secret disturbances."[33] Among the instructions on disturbances are ways of working with physical illness with inner heat practices and yantra yoga exercises. These teachings also discuss disturbances "relating to our view," "relating to our meditation practice," and "relating to our activities."

The third type of instruction covers the practice of the Clear Light. These teachings include practices related to "view," the use of Tsa-lung practices (the yantra yoga of psychic channels, psychic energies, and the essence drops known as "bindus," utilizing various breathing practices, positions, and movements), and the conditions and ways that experiences arise, particularly that of "Clear Light."

The text discusses the types of experiences that arise from practice and the signs of completing the path, specifically the realization of the qualities of abiding in the Natural State. According to this teaching, there are twenty-one signs: nine external, nine internal, and three secret.

The external signs mostly concern the healthy condition of the physical body. They also include the desire to meditate more than take action. Our speech reflects the deepest integrity and most profound view, without words becoming expressions of the Dharmakaya.

The nine internal signs revolve around our experiences and perceptions. For example, we may not notice our breathing, spontaneously have compassion for others, and have less intense emotions, less confusion, and less compelling thoughts. We are able to perceive the insubstantial nature of phenomena and can remain unattached. No matter what we feel, we do not experience suffering and our life is infused with bliss.

Finally, the three secret signs relate to the level of practitioner. The master practitioner is able to reside in the Natural State without being caught up in a lesser condition. The "intermediate practitioner experiences clarity and awareness everywhere, internally and externally, and remains in the Natural State."[34] The less developed practitioner experiences less agitation and finds that thoughts more quickly and naturally dissolve rather than grabbing his or her attention.

In the Buddhist and Bön Dzogchen teachings, there is often emphasis on three kinds of teachings and practice. The first, *rushan*, concerns making the distinction between our habits of thought and the Nature of Mind. The Nature of Mind is described as being like the mirror, and the mind, its thoughts, and processes, are like the reflections in the mirror. The practices of these teachings enable the practitioner to discover this distinction not simply as an intellectual understanding, but as an experienced reality.

The practices often deal with the typical habits of contracted thinking, feeling, acting, and seeking, which are called the realms of suffering. Six realms are distinguished. Each is a fixated, more or less coherent way of viewing reality, having an identity, and behaving based on those views. In a realm we see the world not as it is, but as we are. (See *Opening the Heart of Compassion,* which I co-authored with Lar Short, for an extended discussion of the six realms of suffering and the dynamics and qualities of our basic wisdom nature.[35])

The practices are designed to penetrate our identification with each realm and its compelling concerns so that we see that they have no inherent reality, that they are not our true nature. In these practices we realize the open nature of our being and the wisdom qualities that naturally arise from that nature.

The second kind of Dzogchen teaching and practice deals with cutting through distractions and releasing all tensions so we directly experience the Natural State and can remain in the Natural State without distraction. This is called *trekchod.* The practice "is mainly concerned with realizing the state of total primordial purity that characterizes the Nature of Mind. . . . The Natural State is like the clear, open, limitless sky devoid of clouds, but at the same time this daytime sky is luminous and clear."[36] The experience of this intrinsic awareness or fundamental state of presence is both open and clear whether thoughts arise or not. In the Dzogchen teachings this is referred to as "the Great Perfection."

The full potentiality of Buddhahood is already wholly present in the Natural State from the very beginning, but in order to bring this latent potentiality into visible manifestation, it is necessary to practice the path to remove the obscurations, both emotional and intellectual, that conceal our true face. The sun may be in the sky all the time, but we do not perceive its face and recognize its presence, because its face is obscured and covered by the clouds. But when the clouds are dissipated, the full presence of the sun is revealed. It is the same with enlightenment.[37]

The third type of teaching and practice that works with the Dzogchen principle leads to the recognition that "everything we see and perceive with our senses is totally perfect just as it is because it is a manifestation of the Nature of Mind, our Natural State. Nothing is lacking in it; it is fine just as it is. There is nothing to change, alter, or modify in it."[38]

The realization of this principle means that we manifest the enlightened energy of the Natural State. Our visions are not visualizations (conceptualized imagery) but arise spontaneously out of our resting in the Natural State and so are immediately perceived as the manifestation of our open, free nature—in the teachings this is called being "self-liberated." These practices are known as *thogal,* or the development of vision. Tenzin Wangyal refers to this as "Crossing Over," emphasizing that we integrate with all that arises. Our experience with thogal further supports our perception that the normal way of seeing the world is insubstantial, thereby reducing the grip of attachments and the power of reactive emotions.

"The dark retreat can also serve as a preparation for death and the experiences in the Bardo [the intermediate state that follows death]. Through our practice, we become familiar with the quality and the nature of the visions that will arise in the Bardo."[39]

4 Clarity and Clear Light

As mentioned earlier, clarity refers to the sense of presence that is open and inclusive. This sense of presence can witness and host everything that arises, and provides a foundation for the realization of Clear Light.

In Clear Light we abide in pure, open awareness that is beyond distinctions. It simply is. In this dimension of awareness, there are no characteristics, and at the same time everything is included. Within the stability of Clear Light, thoughts, feelings, and experiences can arise and do not disturb the presence of our awareness beyond all phenomena.

5 Practices of Introduction to Dark Retreat

For short dark retreats, Tenzin Wangyal Rinpoche suggests that the most important goal be relaxation—relaxing the body, the mind, and the momentum of everyday life. In this relaxation we release the grip of tensions and habits into a more open way of being. In a sense, in spiritual development, when everything is released, we achieve liberation.

The *sadhana,* or basic practice, for these initial retreats consists of purification breathing, securing the boundary of the mind, guru yoga, refuge, bodhicitta, contemplative breathing, forced introduction to the lights, unification of three spaces (skies), gazing positions when needed, and dedication. Many of these practices can be found in appendix A.

The four sessions of practice per day—early morning, morning, afternoon, and evening—are gradually expanded in length as our capacity increases. Between sessions it is recommended that one do mindfulness practices, chanting, and resting. The day is concluded with a practice associated with Yeshe Walmo, a protector of the teachings and of the mind.

The core practice for these retreats is the contemplative breathing (see appendix A), which contains the essence of Dzogchen practice. In this practice we move our attention into an essence drop of energy and awareness (thigle in Tibetan, or bindu in Sanskrit) that contains our self-sense, move the thigle through the side channels into the central channel, allow it to float up through the central channel, shoot it out the crown into space, and let it dissolve and finally abide in that dissolution. In the dissolution an open, clear state can occur and the mind of Clear Light can manifest. Abiding in this Clear Light state we rest in the foundation of all awareness and all experience. This is known as the "nature of mind."

Part V
Blessings of Grace

1 Grief and Praise: Selections from Journals of Retreats in 1999 and 2000

Avalokiteshvara drops two tears in my eyes
To see the pain in the world.
The river of grief carves great canyons in my heart
To hold it all
And still there is more.
Yet the beauty of those vast wounds
Transforms everything
Into the boundless radiance of an open landscape.

—Martin Lowenthal, Dark Retreat 2001

In the years since the dark retreat in February 1998, I have done more dark retreats generally lasting for two weeks. A retreat in 1999 was necessarily delayed and shortened by the passing of my mother and one in 2000 ran for two weeks. Although practice was at the core of both these retreats, the context for me was more about exploring and working with the qualities of grief, praise, and transition in my work in the world.

The continuous consciousness of the 1998 retreat persisted for about ten days and then became more periodic in my everyday life. I have been able to access the qualities of resting in pure being, in the nature of Essence (Mind), and the bliss states much more easily, frequently, and for longer periods in the midst of normal life. I also found that simply entering a retreat, not only a dark retreat, would rapidly bring me home to resting in pure being and consciousness. This has been true for the practice retreats I have led for my students and for the dark retreats I have done on my own.

The selections that follow are from my journals of dark retreats in 1999 and 2000.

Dark Retreat April 1999

During the first morning, I experience the profound stillness, silence, and open awareness. Sense of being in heart.

Being here and everywhere simultaneously.

I slept only a few hours last night and yet feel awake, rested, and alert.

Very quickly feeling at home in the dark.

Alertness—sense of open hosting, vibrant awareness is already here. Almost as if I am picking up from the retreat last year.

This is not so much a practice retreat as an opportunity to vacate everyday life to let the dynamics within me to deepen and shape me after Mom's death.

Grieving for Mom. Memories from childhood.

Celebrating her ordinary human qualities and her extraordinary qualities.

My celebration of Mom vibrates my heart and in my being, as if in response to my celebration; it is a mutual praising, a meeting that resonates in the chambers of my soul. And I keep returning to the experience of my breath and the pervasive silence, space, and stillness of the dark. The energy of praise, the radiance of relating opens a space in which presence can simply be. Then my praise feels reciprocated as if the praise of all being sings me into existence.

> Taking inventory in my life:
> blessings
> callings
> strengths
> weaknesses
> directions
> where I am now
> relation to my own existence and gift of life
> my thresholds
> to becoming an elder
> new stage in relationship with Karen
> head of family
> as a spiritual being
> as a teacher
> as a friend

In the darkness of the unknown, the seed of each moment is being grown fresh. It is the wondrous dark unknown of our soul that is germinating what is alive in us—the new beauty. Germination happens in darkness. Seeds will not grow if left in the light of day.

Awoke early from conscious sleep with pervasive sense of presence. During morning nap between practices did dream yoga. I would change the colors in the dream image. Would open my eyes and it would continue for a time. Some images became still shots and others remained in motion.

In one dream of a woman I experimented with touch. As I touched her feet to my arm, it changed and I was feeling the naked flesh of Karen snuggling and moving in my arms and against my body. The sensations, particularly in my arms, were so real. I checked my physical arms as I slept and they were still. The arms with all the sensations were another set, as if I had an extra body. In other parts of the dream, I intentionally tasted some food and smelled the fragrance of a flower.

Day 2

Profound vibrant stillness. Resonant silence and radiant darkness.

Paradoxically, as a teacher, I feel released to a large extent of the need to teach. I can also see the posturing and presentation of self and the attached identities of my being in the role of teacher and author. Not that I will not continue to teach and write. I am coming from a different ground of being.

Many of the creative, formative, and connective dynamics and energies of life are often called spirits and gods. We must honor and feed them by our presence and attention, by creating beauty, and by celebration and praise. If we neglect them, these generative energies can devour us as their impulse to manifest tries to find expression through our layers of numbness, reaction, unconsciousness, and denial.

It is remarkable how many observations become clearer in the dark. It is as though the light of day is too bright and there is more in the field of vision than can be seen and digested. Like food at a seven-course banquet, the taste is lost in quantity. Subtlety may be noted momentarily only to be forgotten and lost in the sheer volume of food and the pace of eating and mindless conversation.

The dark can slow everything down for those who meet its imposing and pervasive atmosphere and who will settle into its rhythms. So much is revealed by letting the senses produce the flow of images, thoughts, and sounds, unimpeded by external stimulation. The world becomes a blank slate of black, silence, and stillness. I am obviously the generator of what arises, along with myriad unseen forces.

Mom's death has encouraged, even forced, me to abide and be in a period of falling away, of silence, and of stillness. Like winter, which clears away and covers what is decayed to provide the layer and conditions for what needs to germinate in the spring of renewal. Often we scrape at and try to melt that covering and prematurely try to force the tender seeds to grow. Our impatience means the flowers are small, the fruit tasteless, and the whole endeavor poorly rooted. I am in that space between winter and spring. I sense new buds emerging as the fluids of meaning, connection, and value rise in my core. Each is still hidden within itself. Each is a prayer seeking nourishment to grow and manifest.

Dark Retreat February 2000

This retreat, like the short one last year, is about both practice and reflection. I note that since the retreat in 1998, I also am more fully and continuously present in my life and clearer in my teaching.

The anniversary of Mom's death will come up toward the end of this retreat. I am opening to the nature and extent of my grief at this time.

Day 3

This morning had a dream that involved elephant/human children. They were crossbreeds. Some were more obviously elephants and others were more human. One, with flesh like a human and wide open, bright eyes had a small trunk-like nose. He was very radiant and totally pleasant. I realized it was Ganesha.

In the dream, the ethical issues of cross-breeding occurred to me. These children had been the result of combining genes of another species with human genes. At the time, this seemed wonderful, in that the purpose was to improve people and breed out the impulse to violence in the extreme, but it also raised issues of playing God, tampering with nature, and the right course for evolution.

At another level I realize as I'm dreaming that this is about another lesson altogether. Where the spirit and the sensory (material) cross makes soul. When we cross the spiritual and material, we give rise to a new possibility, a new mysterious being. As a new being we have an obligation to live what we have learned from our soul journeys.

Sense of presencing. Pure presence—not mine or other—just presence. When thoughts and sensations arose, it was in the space of presencing. I feel clear, calm, and creative. Again I sense being shaped by this process of retreat and by forces I can only sense but do not know.

We practice mindfulness until we or something shifts and natural mindfulness is recognized. This natural mindfulness or presence is not achieved or created. It arises from our beings when the mind gets out of the way.

Day 6

During a late morning meditation, I felt a wave of sadness for and memories of Mom. I realized that the last full day we spent together before her fatal fall was a year ago today. I let it all come in a very open heart space. The images, memories, feelings, and tears all came. For hours I was shaken and shaped by grief.

My grief included ways I had hurt my mother, ways I had missed out by not being with her more later in her life when she was more available, ways I had disappointed her (though she would never have said so), ways I honored her, ways I brought her joy, ways I loved and love her, ways we connected, ways we enjoyed each other and respected each other, what she could not give me and what she did.

I better understood many of my own patterns, good and bad, which I took on from her. This included her difficulty in grieving properly. She did not dwell on pain or loss and did not openly grieve. This is an old Jewish family pattern from my grandparents and before them of carrying on in the face of so much pain and loss. The challenge was to live and make a world of meaning and keep the community alive.

We both tended to keep busy, perhaps too busy. She stopped that when she retired at the age of eighty-two. That is when she blossomed in a new and special way.

My grieving her also brought up other losses and grief from other relationships. I can see that I need to spend more time with many people. The only person I have balance with is Karen.

In my relationship with Karen, which grows closer over the years, I can see the influence of a third force. In intimate relationships there is the ideal of the alchemical wedding, the bringing together of different, often opposite elements to create a third, new element of great value. In turn the individuals emerge in a new way. In a sense, there are three new things. Intimate relationships with others and with the Divine are ways to evoke and manifest the qualities that lie dormant in the soul.

Losses and wounds are often psychic gains if we know how to attend to them and relate to them. They then become something beneficial that we have to share with others and that we can bring to intimacy in a relationship. In this process it is vital that we not create enemies—of others, ourselves, or our wounds. These losses and wounds temper the sword of fierceness and strength, qualities of authentic wisdom. (This is not to be confused with reactive hostility and intense feeling.)

Day 7

Awoke with a sense of presence and presencing. Mindful, open-heart presence is now baseline. It is a flick of attention away—no effort. It is as though everything arises in the space of the heart. The silence of this awareness reveals not only any mind chatter but a general static energy of the mind even when not thinking, the noise of the impulse to think. When we lose the sense of silence, the tendency toward agitation often prevails.

Day 8

There was a wonderful sense of community last night while the group met in the meditation hall and I meditated here in the retreat room.

I am never sure how to describe the full nature of the experience and nature of presence. I will make another attempt, hoping this might add something to my previous articulations. During meditation, eating, and simply being present in a conscious way, I have the sense of pure presencing and it seems connected with all presence. As I experience sensation, thoughts, feelings, tastes, etc., these experiences are transformed, or their energy, their qualities of presence, their value is radiated or shared by all presence. In other words, it is not just personal. It becomes a beneficial part of larger wholes, of community, of all being. It is like the heart space is a zone of being connected to all being. The energy of life is liberated from the confines of the personality into a vast space transcending location and time. It takes each moment into the beyond. It carries the radiance into the vastness of all life and spirit.

In addition, this is a great feedback system in which I am being worked by these phenomena. I am not making any of it happen. It simply is. And I am being shaped and molded by it.

In this formation process, I sense my physical, mental, and emotional bodies are being transformed into a dedication body—a body of light and presence that is fully sensory and also completely soulful and Spirit.

I am fully loved and embraced and fully loving and embracing. My essence is dancing with, kissing, stroking, and merging with Essence, All Being. Not just the Essence, but all the essences, the gods and goddesses that bring forth life, and nourish us and the world.

During a dream in a nap, a tiger's face suddenly appeared. We stared eye to eye. In the process I sensed a gift was transmitted to me. I don't know what, but it is in my being. I was fully conscious in the dream and thanked the tiger and the face transformed into a bear and another gift was transmitted. Again I thanked the bear. Then another transformation. The eyes became hollow and the face bony. This was the face of death. Again some great gift was transmitted into me. I felt a quickening and thanked death. The face faded and there was simply space.

I had opened my eyes in the dark as the dream continued and I slept. After the last face had appeared, I continued my sleep with my eyes closed. Upon awakening from the nap, the sense of wonder filled my sense of being.

One of the most important preparations for death is letting go of things in life when the time is right. We use the everyday process of living and dying, of going through cycles, to sensitize and train us to die well and consciously.

Day 10

Reflected on the pain and deaths of those in the various holocausts of the past century, included the German against the Jews, the Turkish against the Armenians, the Cambodian against Cambodians, and the Hutu against the Tutsis. I also reflected on the survivors and the triumph of their spirit to carry on, to live and create life. I wept. All these people inspire me. My tears are my sadness, gratitude, love, and my heart being touched. My tears are my offering and dedication.

It is the wound that opens us to the world. It can also mean we feel separated from others. This separation is the basis of fragmentation, but also can result in a coming together. The wound is the challenge to create benefit and beauty. Healing is making whole through the process and experiencing the wonder of connection.

In my reflections, I recalled how gods come to us in many forms, often in disguises to test our responses—the story of Rosalita who goes to the well: An old, ragged, poor, crippled woman comes and asks Rosalita to draw water for her. Rosalita says certainly and does so. The goddess reveals herself and says to Rosalita that henceforth when she speaks, diamonds and rubies and emeralds will come forth. And it is so. Rosalita goes home and tells her stepmother, who sends her own daughters to the well. She tells them to give the hag whatever she wants. They go off grumbling and wait at the well with envy and hatred in their hearts at their stepsister. A distinguished, well-dressed woman wearing jewels appears and asks them to draw some water for her. They look at her with a disdainful air and say, "Draw it yourself." The goddess then condemns them to have lizards and bugs come from their mouths.

Day 11

Arose early and did a long memorial meditation for Mom. This is the anniversary of her passing last year. In the meditation I opened my heart as completely as I know how and let memories, images, feelings, grief, love, gratitude, inspiration, etc., arise. I maintained a dignified meditative presence as all these swept through me. My eyes kept watering the garden of my heart. I even wailed for a time, something that has not blessed me since childhood.

As before, the grief and love and praise for my father came as well. And so did that for my grandparents and other relatives. Then the love for all my living family. Everybody dear to me touched and broke my heart. And every person became dear to me (even people I don't care for). Suddenly they were so real, so human and alive. My heart exploded, reaching out and giving a home to everybody and all the love.

I did a radiating meditation where I gathered all my love, gratitude, joy, respect, admiration, inspiration, and radiance; pulled it into my heart center from all parts of my body, being, and beyond; and radiated it to the heart of my mother, father, and others. I picture them in front of me, just above eye level.

She (and they) received this luminous energy, assimilated it, and in turn radiated it out from their hearts to their loved ones, friends, etc. Each in turn did the same, reaching all beings and filling all space with loving, thankful, joyous, inspiring, radiantly luminous energy.

We are called upon to be a medium, to stand in the middle between the sacred and the sensory, to bring Spirit to life and livingness to the invisible spirit. We do this as individuals, couples, families, communities, and as a species. We bring the nourishment of love and value and presence to this sensory, material world, and we present the beauty we create in life to the invisible world of the spirit.

The core forces and experiences of life cannot be comprehended by the neurological brain; they cannot be captured by a concept. Only our whole being (which includes our body) can work with and be worked by these mighty, divinely immense phenomena. We can only recognize them through mystical images, an otherworldly voice, and ecstatic movement. Even then we need not so much to express what they are as be shaped by them— become a medium for them in life and relationships. Our practice is partly to develop our mediumistic capacity, our ability to be on that edge and act in the middle, in the intersection and interaction of the world and the spirit.

We need to be open to being moved by the awesome forces of life, death, the earth, the larger stories that we are a part of, by the wisdom energies of gods and goddesses, who can be flesh-ripping in their ferocity. Only by being consumed by the flames of life can we be reborn and grow into maturity, wisdom, and love.

A major ingredient in conscious maturing is being able to hold experiences and what we come to know. Holding means not judging or reacting. This includes pain, unknowns, injustices, conflicting feelings, competing desires, the ungovernable forces of our nature, of relationships, of larger nature, of life, and of the Divine. It is our lot to carry what we cannot comprehend, to use what we did not choose and don't like, and to create benefit and value from nothing.

Being conscious often makes our hearts ache, our heads ache, and our backs ache. Our hearts because we are constantly challenged to break open and connect to beauty, pain, love, loss, destruction, and death. Our heads because we want to understand and manage what is incomprehensible and unpredictable. Our backs because we must carry all of life anyway and create beauty and meaning from our burdens. The heart must hold the fact that its task is to apprehend what cannot be fully apprehended. It is paradoxical that holding this fact gives us a way of being with it all—of being present.

Blessing means to strengthen someone by investing them with

resources from the Divine. This way God's strength flows through us. We want to find the blessing in each situation—what will give us strength and spirit and courage.

This evening, quiet thoughts and images simply pass by like occasional clouds to decorate a clear sky. Sequential time passes mostly unnoticed as I am living beyond time.

Day 13

Last full day of this retreat in the dark. Tomorrow is a transition day.

Arose early after a night of conscious sleep. My last dream, which I kept extending my sleep to somehow complete, was quite unusual. In the long and complex sequence of it, there were constant transformations and integration of life forces and opposites, the transformation of life into death into life.

The dream included an adventurer who swims among crocodiles. They attack him but he transforms into a croc himself and plays with them, and later transforms back to a man. In the dream I am both the main character and a witness who knows more than my character.

In another part of the dream, I casually enter the apartment of a woman I do not know in order to look at some oriental art books on her desk. As I examine them, she appears in another part of the apartment to get something and notices me there. She is not startled (though I expect her to be). After stating my reasons for being there, she comes over to me and gives me teachings on sacred art. She is an Asian artist and very supportive, open, and instructive.

As the dream progresses, I have a wife (whom I cannot identify) and we are traveling to some part of France, somehow in search of a lost child we believe has died. We stop at a town where a famous priest named Father Jean has a church. As we approach the church, services are finishing and streams of people are leaving—thousands. As we make our way in, my wife and I are one—I am both, though I do not fully realize it yet. Inside the sanctuary it is completely empty—no pews, no altars, no pictures, no objects, no cloth, no pulpit. It is a great open womb with arched ceilings and alcoves. There is plenty of light, but no windows and no candles or light fixtures.

I go to find Father Jean even while the witness part knows that

Father Jean is a woman. As I search the living quarters adjacent to the church, I know that Father Jean has children and has lost a child. There are children playing happily in a room in the house. I still do not consciously know that Father Jean is a woman. I come to Father Jean's room and am about to enter when I see the priest slipping into a free-standing bathtub. As the robes come off, a woman's body is unveiled. I am too embarrassed to enter.

I slip up a stairway to a private meditation room, trying to go unnoticed. Shortly, she comes up the stairs drying her hair. As she enters the room, she draws the towel from her face and she sees me. She is totally naked and very beautiful. She is surprised by my presence but casually slips into a loose, comfortable robe or kaftan and comes to be with me. She is completely pleasant and welcoming. She explains that her name is Jeanine. She says she is both Father and Mother, in both priestly and physical ways. I realize I am both husband and wife at that moment. I have so many questions and we sit and have a conversation. She asks about me and I about her. I have the sense of having entered the realm of goddesses and gods. I am given teachings and blessings. I have a profound sense of the beauty and wonder of life.

I awake before I have asked all my questions, but this is right since our relationship is secure and ongoing. Now there is no hurry, only gratitude, joy, and dedication.

Appendix A
Practices for Dark Retreat

I have included selected practices in this appendix that can be done in the light as part of daily practice, as well as in the dark. These practices are fairly simple to learn and require effort to master. It is advisable that you find a qualified teacher to guide you in your own meditation practice. It is not recommended that you try to undertake a dark retreat without appropriate preparation, and it is very important to have a teacher to guide and support you.

Purification Breathing

Purpose
1. To move attention along the core channel.

2. To open the central and side energy channels.

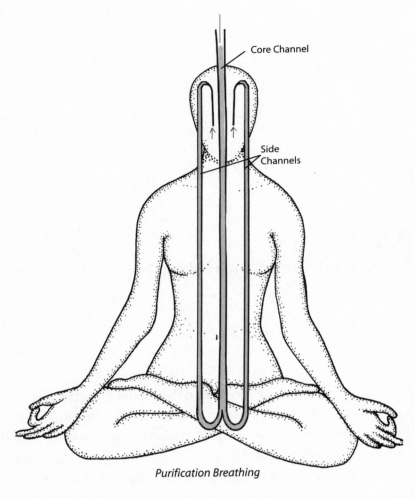

Purification Breathing

3. To release contracted feelings, emotions, and impulses.

4. To radiate wisdom energy.

Set-Up

1. Sit up in a way that the crown of your head is aligned over your perineum (the area between the genitals and the anus) so that you are relaxed, alert, and can breathe easily.

2. Place your hands in your lap or on your legs with your thumbs and index fingers touching.

3. Visualize the three hollow channels in the core of the body. The side channels to the right and left begin at the nostrils, curve up around under the skull, and drop vertically down through the core of the body and join with the central channel just above the perineum. The central channel is straight and rises up through the center and opens at the crown of the head.

First Set of Three Breaths

1. Raise the right hand with the thumb pressing the base of the ring finger. Inhale through the left nostril while closing the right nostril with the ring finger. Then exhale through the right nostril while closing the left nostril with the ring finger. End the exhalation with a rapid push of the diaphragm. Imagine that the inhalation is drawn down through the left-side channel and exhaled up through the right-side channel and out the nostril into a radiant field on the right side. Repeat this for three inhalations and exhalations.

2. During each exhalation, all impulses, confusions, and tensions related to fear, anxiety, aversion, anger, frustration, struggle, and aggression are expressed through the right channel and nostril as smoky-gray soot dissolving into and radiating pure white light of lovingkindness and participation.

Second Set of Three Breaths

1. Raise the left hand with the thumb pressing the base of the ring finger. Inhale through the right nostril while closing the left nostril with the ring finger. Then exhale through the left nostril while closing the right nostril with the ring finger. Imagine that the inhalation is drawn down through the right-side channel and exhaled up through the

left-side channel and out the nostril into a radiant field on the left side. Repeat this for three inhalations and exhalations.

2. During each exhalation, all impulses, confusions, and tensions related to neediness, wanting, desire, clinging, addiction, attachment, scarcity, and worry are expressed through the left channel and nostril as red-black, burgundy soot dissolving into and radiating pure red light of gratitude and contribution.

Third Set of Three Breaths

1. With the hands on your lap, inhale through both nostrils. Then exhale through both nostrils. Imagine that the inhalation is drawn down through both side channels and exhaled up through the central core channel and out the top of the head into a radiant field in the center and all around. Repeat this for three inhalations and exhalations.

2. During each exhalation, all impulses, confusions, and tensions related to ignorance, blame, avoidance, indifference, numbness, and blind pride are expressed through the core channel and the top of the head as navy blue soot dissolving into and radiating pure lapis blue light of respect and aim.

Core Channel Breathing

Purpose

1. To place our attention and self sense in an essence drop of being—bindu—in the central channel, the middle of the core channels, which runs through the central axis of the body, a little nearer the back than the front.

2. To move the essence drop through the central channel, enhancing our sense of this channel, opening it, and clearing the channel from our base to a point beyond our crown.

Core Channel Breathing

Set-Up

1. Sit up in a way that the crown of your head is aligned over your perineum so that you are relaxed, alert, and can breathe easily.

2. Place your hands in your lap or on your legs with your thumbs and index fingers touching.

3. In this meditation sense an essence drop of being—self-sense—at the base in the central channel. Sense the channel running from your

perineum through the core of your body, out the crown to a blue star about an arm's length above your head.

Clearing and Balancing the Core

1. Inhale through your mouth, very softly making the sound "ahhh."

2. As you inhale, an essence drop, a white bindu, ascends from the perineum, your core base, to above your head. Sense your attention moving up the center of your body as the essence drop ascends. Sense the coolness of the ascension. As it leaves your head, the bindu goes around a blue star.

3. As the bindu goes around the blue star it turns blue, as you very softly say "hummm" in the transition from the inhalation to the exhalation.

4. Exhale slowly. As the bindu descends it turns red, becomes warm, and moves through the middle core channel, the same channel it ascended. Throughout the descent say "hreeeee" (phonetically spelled) with an exaggerated smile.

5. When the bindu reaches your base, pause briefly as your breath transitions from the exhalation to the inhalation, and repeat the process.

Contemplative Breathing

Visualize the three hollow channels in the core of the body. The side channels to the right and left begin at the nostrils, curve up around under the skull, drop vertically down through the center of the body, and join with the central channel at an opening just below the navel. The central channel is straight and rises up through the center and opens at the crown of the head.

Contemplative Breathing

1. Close your eyes, exhale stale air, and relax. Then slowly inhale light green flows of energy through the two nostrils. Visualize that these flows pass downward through the side channels and inflate them like a balloon. When the flows reach the place where all three channels join, they are transformed into a single, luminous white drop. This represents your own innate awareness.

2. Gently hold your breath while you imagine this luminous white

essence drop moving with a floating quality upward through the blue central channel. When it reaches the throat area, you begin to exhale slowly, causing the essence drop to move more quickly to the top of your head. Then continue with a more intense exhalation, shooting the essence drop through the crown of your head. When it reaches about a foot in its upward flight, it dissolves into space and your eyes gently open and gaze softly into space. As the essence drop melts into space, your own innate awareness and space become unified.

3. Abide in this state of clarity, not changing anything as long as the experience remains fresh and your mind does not get caught up in thoughts that arise.

4. When you find your attention is no longer open and is following a train of thought, close your eyes and repeat the breathing and visualization again.

Mindfulness Breathing

Purpose
1. To develop the capacity to witness in the moment without commentary.

2. To train the attention and develop both concentration and decentration.

3. To gain greater consciousness of sensations, subtle energies, and other dimensions of being.

4. To enhance your sense of presence.

Set-Up
1. Sit up in a way that the crown of your head is aligned over your perineum so that you are relaxed, alert, and can breathe easily.

2. Place your hands in your lap or on your legs with your thumbs and index fingers touching, or clasp them together, right hand on top, and place them in your lap.

Witnessing Sensations

1. Begin by establishing the sense of being a hosting presence. Notice the sensations in your hands. As you experience some tingling or pulsing sensations in your hands, also place some of your attention on the sensation of your breathing. Hear sounds. Listen not only with your ears, but with your whole body. Listen particularly from the back of the head. Have a sense of listening not only to the sounds, but to the silence in which the sounds arise. Notice that thoughts come and go, and that the feelings as they arise, pass on through and disappear. Experience yourself hosting the sensations, the listening, the thoughts, and the feelings. Host everything that arises. In this hosting, sense yourself as the connection between heaven and earth and as convergence of the three treasures of the skylike spaciousness of generative openness, of the earth power for rich, nourishing manifestation, and of the relational power of your heart reaching out and including all humanity and living beings connecting you to all life.

2. Inhale through the nose and experience the sensations of the breath in the nose, throat, trachea, and into your chest.

3. Sense drawing the breath into your heart center in the middle of your chest, feeling that center opening and expanding.

4. On the exhalation, let your attention expand outward from your heart center, noticing the sensations in the rest of your body and beyond. This is like experiencing the radiance emanating from your heart center as it expands throughout your body and into your aura and on out into the universe.

5. As you continue, open your eyes (if they are not already) with a soft gaze, promoting a sense of spacious presence in the world.

6. Close your meditation by dedicating your practice to the happiness, growth, and freedom of all living beings, radiating the benefits in all directions.

Tonglen: Receiving and Sending

Purpose

When we open to growing through our own pain and grief, we can sense being part of a larger community of people who suffer. We cultivate our courage, dignity, and willingness to experience that aspect of the human condition. We recognize that our own desire to live beyond pain and to be happy is true for others. We can relate to their situation. The sense of space and beneficial intention to realize our personal and collective wisdom nature leads us to wanting to do something about the suffering of others and to open beyond our tendency towards self-preoccupation. As we move beyond our self-concern and our reactive emotions, we realize that we may actually be capable of bringing some sense of freshness, warmth, kindness, and encouragement to the atmosphere that others experience.

This meditation is designed to open our hearts to others and to share the benefits of our practice to create a more supportive and loving environment for everybody. Often we are most resourceful when we are helping someone else in distress. This process combines this impulse with a sense of basic goodness to cultivate a radiance that not only benefits others, but paradoxically us as well, as we actively dedicate ourselves to the benefit of all beings.

The simple exercise of sending and receiving can develop the qualities of relationship and compassion. It uses the capacity of your heart to digest the energy of suffering and transform it into aliveness in yourself and others.

Set-Up

1. Sit up in a way that the crown of your head is aligned over your perineum so that you are relaxed, alert, and can breathe easily.

2. Place your hands in your lap or on your legs with your thumbs and index fingers touching or clasp them together, right hand on top, and place them in your lap.

Receiving and Sending

1. Begin by establishing the sense of being a hosting presence. Notice the sensations in your hands. As you experience some tingling or pulsing sensations in your hands, also place some of your attention on the sensation of your breathing. Hear sounds. Listen not only with your ears, but with your whole body. Listen particularly from the back of the head. Have a sense of listening not only to the sounds, but to the silence in which the sounds arise. Notice that thoughts come and go, and that the feelings as they arise, pass on through and disappear. Experience yourself hosting the sensations, the listening, the thoughts, and the feelings. Host everything that arises. In this hosting, sense yourself as the connection between heaven and earth and as convergence of the three treasures of the skylike spaciousness of generative openness, of the earth power for rich, nourishing manifestation, and of the relational power of your heart reaching out and including all humanity and living beings connecting you to all life.

2. Picture a jewel in your heart center.

3. Think of something that you suffer from and realize that there are other beings who are suffering in a similar way.

4. Sensing the jewel in your heart, breathe in your pain and that of all

beings. Realize that, if it were possible, you would give your life to remove all the suffering in the world. Hold your breath as you hold that suffering in the jewel in your heart.

5. Feel the pressure of your held breath and of your heart center breaking the suffering down into its essential energy.

6. Bring to mind your sense of hosting, love, and caring, feeling your heart being saturated with those qualities and the jewel in your heart becoming ever more radiant from the intensity of your beneficial desire and your feelings. You are making your heart center into a transformer and a generator of value.

7. Radiate that sense of hosting, love, and caring as energy and light to the hearts of all beings.

8. After practicing with the held breath for a few minutes, continue the practice with relaxed breathing, staying conscious that every inhalation is touching your heart with the human condition, and every exhalation is radiating freshness, hosting, love, and caring energy and light.

Appendix B
A Dark Retreat of Your Own

For those interested in doing a dark retreat, I recommend that you find a qualified teacher to prepare and guide you through the process. This is particularly true of any extended retreat and any retreat using tantric or Dzogchen practices. If you are experienced with meditation and have a sense of stability with mindfulness practices, doing a two- to three-day retreat on your own can be very useful. Using flotation tanks that are dark can also be helpful in giving you a glimpse of some of the initial experiences that arise in the dark, particularly relaxation, openness, and seeing inner lights. These short retreats do not develop the stability of consciousness and the capacities that prepare us for the arising of Clear Light and the ability to realize and embody that quality beyond the retreat. Only in extended retreats do certain experiences arise and do we have the time and support for cultivating the wisdom qualities that truly transform our body of habits.

Inner Preparations

1. The inner preparation involves both teachings and practices that open our attention and release what we think we know. We want to become so versed in the teachings that we do not think about them.

2. Begin more intensive practice about a week before doing a significant retreat, reviewing instructions that will be incorporated into the retreat practices. Get whatever specific instructions your teacher has for you far enough in advance that you have time to practice them prior to your retreat. Also clarify any questions you may have.

3. Your mindset and attitude upon entering the retreat can set the stage for your experiences in the retreat. It would be great to enter with a sense of clarity, openness, joy, and resting in your true nature, but this is more the fruit of the retreat than a prerequisite. Some of the attitudes I have found useful are: looking forward to a wonderful rest and vacation from the pressures of everyday life; curiosity about what will arise; longing to get the clarity, wisdom, and fruits of doing the practices and the retreat; dedication to growth; treating whatever arises as an opportunity to learn; connection to my teachers and the teachings; sense of support from the community; service to the larger community and the world, and wanting to be a beneficial presence; confidence from the fact that others have successfully navigated through such retreats for thousands of years and brought back treasures from their efforts; and gratitude for this opportunity to learn, grow, and create benefit and beauty for yourself, others, and the world.

4. There is also one other important quality that you want to have in your journey—a sense of humor. Taking yourself very seriously creates enormous barriers to relaxing into your nature and opening to the unknown.

Practical Preparations

1. Make sure the retreat space is light-tight. This requires spending thirty to forty minutes in the room in the dark before the retreat. It takes about that amount of time for the eyes to adjust and our perception to become sensitive enough to detect even the faintest light leaks from the outside.

2. Have a system of adequate ventilation in place. In our dark retreat space there is a specially designed intake vent to the outdoors. This unit has sufficient turns in it to prevent any light from being reflected into the room. It also has a very quiet inverted fan at the interior part of the opening to draw fresh air into the retreat space. There is a switch on the wall to turn this fan on and off. We also have an exhaust fan in the bathroom that is turned on periodically during the day to expel the stale air and any odors from the space.

3. Lay out your clothes and other items so that you can easily determine where they are. Creating and remembering the organization of all your things makes everyday functioning much easier.

4. Use thick black electrical tape on the lighted indicators of any electrical equipment you may need such as a heater or humidifier. If you know how, simply disconnect the wires to the lights in such equipment.

5. Set up reliable caretaking arrangements so that you do not need to worry about food or other everyday matters outside of the retreat space and time. Involving other people in your retreat helps to weave together the fabric of your spiritual community and to give others the opportunity to share in the retreat through their service.

6. Of course, one of the critical matters is taking care of business before entering the retreat. For those of us who do not live in monasteries—who have family and work obligations, and have many responsibilities that are not generally shared—this can be challenging.

Practices

Begin your practices with some simple clearing and balancing of your mind and the energies of your body. Hold your intention and purpose for your practice and your retreat in your mind and your heart. Connect with your teacher(s) and all wisdom forces, thanking them for their presence and asking for their support in your practice. Invoke their wisdom qualities and energies, inviting them to gather in your heart center. Sense yourself manifesting these qualities as you begin your practice.

Besides the practices that you have been instructed to do in the retreat, you may find that you need to do more stabilizing and mindfulness practices than you may have anticipated. Insert these as needed.

In closing the practice sessions, call on the background alert part of your mind to notice when you are getting distracted, agitated, or reactive, so that it can remind you to be consciously present. In the Tibetan tradition this is done using protector deities such as the Bön deity, Yeshe Walmo.

Close each session with a dedication of the benefits of the practice. We do not simply work for ourselves, making the value dependent on our situations and memories. In dedicating the merits of our work to others, we transmit the qualities and energies that resulted from practice into the world so that others can receive them and carry on the value. This amplifies the effect and keeps the work alive.

The dedication shifts attention to the world around us integrating the external with our internal practice. The sights, sounds, and events that occur then become stimuli for extending our conscious work beyond formal practice. In the relaxed space of meditating in the dark, everything that arises becomes a reminder of openness and the desire to remain alert and present. Everything becomes a support for practice. All sounds are the voice of wisdom. All visions are the expressions of clarity. And all sensations are the caress of presence.

Centers to Do Dark Retreat

Dedicated Life Institute (under the direction of Martin Lowenthal)
53 Westchester Road
Newton, MA 02458
617-527-8606
mldli@rcn.com
www.dli.org

Ligmincha Institute (under the direction of Tenzin Wangyal Rinpoche)
P.O. Box 1892
Charlottesville, VA 22903
434-977-6161
ligmincha@aol.com
www.ligmincha.org

Tsegyalgar (under the direction of Choegyal Namkhai Norbu)
The Dzogchen Community
18 School House Road
Conway, MA 01341
413-369-4153
fax: 413-369-4165
74404.1141@compuserve.com
www.tashi.org/tsegyalgar

Endnotes

1. *Ngöndro* is the set of "preliminary" practices that are considered preparation for advanced work in tantra and Dzogchen. They are a way to dissolve the patterns of reactive habits and to create the inner conditions for wisdom to arise. They begin the process of retraining ways of thinking, feeling, and relating so that we can become clear of old patterns, can use the teachings and our teachers as guides and connections to the blessings of wisdom, and can dedicate our lives to the realization of wisdom for the benefit of all beings.

2. Guru yoga involves visualizing the teacher as an embodiment of the wisdom of Buddha. The teacher becomes both an example of the enlightened state and an inspiration for our own desire to fully realize ourselves as wisdom beings. The guru as mentor transmits the teachings, instructs us on their application, and guides us on our own path of spiritual development. The practice of guru yoga provides us with a link to the sacred dimensions of wisdom. As Robert Thurman points out in his book *Essential Tibetan Buddhism,* the culture of Tibet is organized around the experience that real Buddhas live among them and their entire society is shaped by the influence of real Buddhas. Individual and social life revolves around opening to the wisdom of these Buddhas, realizing the possibility of becoming one oneself, and working with proven methods passed down through the ages for realizing this potential in ourselves.

3. *Zhiné (shamatha)* practices develop concentration so that we may develop the capacity for calm abiding, a state of open, fresh peacefulness. This state initially

takes effort. After extended practice we cultivate the ability to simply relax into this state and eventually to be stable in the state, so that it persists and can host whatever phenomena arise. The development of this calm abiding provides a foundation for all other meditation practices.

4. *Vipashyana (Vipassana)* practices develop clarity so that we recognize our true nature and the nature of all existence—namely, impermanence, suffering, and that which is beyond our thoughts, feelings, identities, and experiences. We come to realize, beyond any intellectual understanding, the open or empty nature of phenomena.

5. Matthew Fox in Fox and Rupert Sheldrake, *Natural Grace,* (New York: Doubleday, 1997), 136.

6. Walt Whitman, "A Clear Midnight" in *Leaves of Grass, and Selected Prose,* (New York: Rinehart, 1943), 398.

7. Matthew Fox, *Original Blessing,* (Santa Fe, N. Mex.: Bear, 1983), 157.

8. T. S. Eliot, "East Coker" in *Four Quartets,* (London: Faber and Faber, 1944), 27.

9. Excerpt from "Sweet Darkness" from *The House of Belonging* by David Whyte. ©1997 by David Whyte. Reprinted with permission of the author and Many Rivers Press.

10. Thomas Cleary and Sartaz Aziz, *Twilight Goddess,* (Boston: Shambhalla, 2000), 138.

11. Ibid., 151.

12. Peter Kingsley, *In the Dark Places of Wisdom,* (Inverness, Calif.: Golden Sufi Center, 1999), 53–54. Reprinted with the permission of the author and The Golden Sufi Center, P.O. Box 428, Inverness, CA 94937, tel. 415-663-8773, email: goldensufi@aol.com, website: www.goldensufi.org.

13. Ibid., 67.

14. Ibid., 71.

15. Ibid., 80.

16. Ibid., 89.

17. Ibid., 102–103.

18. Reprinted from *Times Alone: Selected Poems* by Antonio Machado, translated by Robert Bly, Wesleyan University Press, Middletown, Conn., 1985. Copyright 1985 by Robert Bly. Reprinted with his permission.

19. Tenzin Wangyal, *The Tibetan Yogas of Dream and Sleep,* (Ithaca, N.Y.: Snow Lion Publications, 1998), 59.

20. Denise Levertov, *Poems 1972–1982,* (New York: New Directions Pub., 2001), 260–61.

21. Excerpt from "The Faces at Braga" from *Where Many Rivers Meet* by David Whyte. ©1990 by David Whyte. Reprinted with permission of the author and Many Rivers Press.

22. See Tarthung Tulku, *Time, Space, and Knowledge: A New Vision of Reality,*

(Emeryville, Calif.: Dharma Pub., 1977); *Knowledge of Time and Space*, (Oakland, Calif.: Dharma Pub., 1990); and *Dynamics of Time and Space*, (Berkeley, Calif.: Dharma Pub., 1994).

23. From author's memory of a talk entitled "Your Solitude Is Luminous" given by John O'Donohue in 1996.

24. Jacob Needleman, *Money and the Meaning of Life*, (New York: Doubleday, 1991), 34.

25. W. B. Yeats, "The Song of Wandering Aengus" in *The Collected Poems of W. B. Yeats,* (New York: The MacMillan Company, 1933), 57.

26. David Wagoner, "Lost," in *Who Shall Be the Sun*, (Bloomington: Indiana Univ. Press, 1978), 5.

27. Tenzin Wangyal, *Wonders of the Natural Mind*, (Ithaca, N.Y.: Snow Lion Publications, 1993), 10–19.

28. Tenzin Wangyal, *Healing with Form, Energy, and Light*, (Ithaca, N.Y.: Snow Lion Publications, 2002), 2.

29. Ibid., 131.

30. Ibid.

31. Ibid., 132.

32. Tenzin Namdak, transcribed and edited by Vajranatha (John Myrdhin Reynolds), *The Instructions of Shardza Rinpoche for the Practice of Vision and the Dark Retreat* from the *rDzogs-chen sku-gsum rangshar,* (Bonpo Translation Project, 1992), 23.

33. Ibid., 29.

34. Ibid., 42.

35. Martin Lowenthal and Lar Short, *Opening the Heart of Compassion: Transform Suffering Through Buddhist Psychology and Practice,* (Boston: C. E. Tuttle, 1993).

36. Namdak, 4.

37. Ibid., 5.

38. Ibid., 6.

39. Ibid., 46.

Index

About the Author

 Martin Lowenthal, Ph.D. is an ordained senior meditation teacher and mentor with the Dedicated Life Institute. Dr. Lowenthal is the author of *Embrace Yes* and co-author of *Opening the Heart of Compassion*. In addition to conducting workshops and retreats internationally, he serves as a pastoral counselor, trainer, consultant, and writer.

He has been on the faculty at Boston College and Harvard University Extension and has studied with Buddhist and Taoist Masters for more than thirty years. His spiritual teachers have included H. H. Dilgo Khyentse Rinpoche, Chogyam Trungpa Rinpoche, Lopon Tenzin Namdak, Tenzin Wangyal Rinpoche, and Lar Short.

Dr. Lowenthal received his doctorate from the University of California, Berkeley in 1970, has worked as an applied anthropologist in Botswana, Africa, and directed a policy research institute from 1970 to 1977.

A practicing psychotherapist, he lives with his wife Karen, in Newton, Massachusetts.

Dedicated Life Institute
Cultivating Wisdom Presence
for Everyday Life

The Dedicated Life Institute (DLI) supports spiritual exploration and growth, and is dedicated to making the Essence teachings of many traditions accessible in a Western idiom. Incorporating the principles of the mystic way, we promote both recovery of our wisdom ground of being and development of our capacity to use our daily conditions as a means of growth and as the opportunity to manifest our true wisdom nature. Our dedication to living as an expression of wisdom serves to encourage both personal and social transformation.

Founded by Martin Lowenthal, the Institute offers meditation groups, retreats, workshops, and a home study program.

For more information, please contact:
Dedicated Life Institute
53 Westchester Road
Newton, Massachusetts 02458
617-527-8606

Visit our web site: www.dli.org
email: mldli@rcn.org

Hampton Roads Publishing Company

... for the evolving human spirit

Hampton Roads Publishing Company
publishes books on a variety of subjects,
including metaphysics, health,
visionary fiction, and other related topics.

For a copy of our latest catalog, call toll-free
(800) 766-8009, or send your name and address to:

Hampton Roads Publishing Company, Inc.
1125 Stoney Ridge Road
Charlottesville, VA 22902

e-mail: hrpc@hrpub.com
www.hrpub.com